Bernetta's Artistic Journey

Bernetta's Artistic Journey

The Life and Work of Bernie DuBois

Jim and Jane,
Thanks for
your many years
of friendship.
Bernetta DuBois

BERNETTA DUBOIS

Fenwick Publishing Group, Inc.

First edition
Printed in China

ISBN: 978-0-9889261-7-2

Fenwick Publishing Group, Inc.
3147 Point White Drive, Suite 100
Bainbridge Island, Washington 98110

Fenwick Publishing develops custom books, videos, apps, and content for global organizations and private individuals or families.

www.fenwickpublishing.com

President: Timothy J. Connolly
Editor: Sarah Morgans
Design Concept: Kevin Berger
Proofreader: Laurie Gibson

CONTENTS

Love is a miracle, sweet as can be,

That will always remain a complete mystery.

For though it is something that's centuries old,

It cannot be purchased for silver or gold.

But instead must be given of one's own free will

And received with no promises that must be fulfilled.

And once it's exchanged in this time-honored way,

There's nothing that love cannot manage to say.

No problem too great and no problem too small,

For love, like a miracle, conquers them all

And leaves in their place such a feeling of peace

That joy, just like love, cannot help but increase!

— unknown

INTRODUCTION

My art has kept me alive.

Writing this book was triggered by my wish to share what I'd creatively produced over the past few decades. To compile the images for the book, I reviewed hundreds of photos of paintings, drawings, and sculptures. Many of them revealed to me that there's been a particular relationship between me and my artwork, one that goes beyond the mere act of rendering each piece. It's not simply been fun. Part of my relationship with my work has come from feeling satisfied that I scrambled up a steep learning curve and tackled new techniques. And yet even beyond that—beyond the fun and the sense of accomplishment—the work has provided me with something special.

For one thing, working on my canvasses or sculptures became, at many times, a marvelous distraction and comfort when I faced bouts of chronic pain. I now also clearly see that my artwork frequently provided a strong thread connecting me to friends, to family members, to my dear, fun, and witty husband and the memories of adventure and travels we have shared.

As such, my art stands as physical representation of the treasured connections I made linking myself to the past. The thread might be paintings done with talented artist friends who have worked by my side, shared their thoughts and feedback, or displayed their work in the same shows—and with whom I remain fast friends. Or the thread might be pieces with which I chose to commemorate people dear to me—either lifelong friends and family or individuals who had a fleeting but important interaction with me that I will always treasure.

All of these things—the fun of doing the artwork, the pride in accomplishing new and challenging techniques, and the connections to memories, friendships, and passions—I hope to have captured in this book. I also hope, in these pages, to ultimately illuminate my statement at the start of this introduction: "My art has kept me alive."

Angels Love Song / Collage / 9" x 12"

Humble Beginnings

1

My twin, Lorie, and I were born into a family of four girls and my parents, Lottie and Herman, shown above at our farm in Pepin, Wisconsin, and at right with our older sisters before we were born.

A Growing Family

In the upper Mississippi River Valley you will find Pepin, Wisconsin, a small town that remains sparsely populated today. Mostly rocky farmland, it took a lot of hard labor to prepare the land for growing crops.

This is where my parents, Lottie and Herman Oebser, lived with four girls, ranging from the ages of six to twelve, when I was born October 26, 1939.

A midwife was present at the time of my birth, made particularly notable by the fact that my mother had just finished giving birth to another girl. It was fifteen minutes later when the midwife said to my parents, "but wait, we think you are going to have twins." That was something that few parents would be prepared to hear.

With twin girls weighing 9 1/2 pounds—my twin weighed 5 pounds and I weighed 4 1/2 pounds—they faced a dilemma. They were not equipped to care for babies so tiny. The only things they had at home that they felt they could safely put us in were shoeboxes. But it was only a matter of time before we were the size of normal babies and could be put in cribs. My mother later admitted that even though we were fraternal, not identical, twins, the family had a problem knowing one of us from the other, so I got a single toenail painted red.

Yet another unexpected challenge for my parents was what to name us. It's never been very clear to me how they came up with the name Bernetta. At that time there were many babies named Loretta, and Bernice and Bernadette were also somewhat popular girls' names

My parents had to wait until Lorie (right) and I were about eighteen months before they could have our portrait taken—they were waiting for my hair to come in!

At my parents' fiftieth wedding anniversary in 1975, celebrated at our farm in Menomonie, my sisters and I took this fun picture. The sexy six are (from left) me, Edith, Irene, Lorie, Lois, and Betty. Facing page, left: We gathered again for a more traditional portrait, this time including my brother and parents, for their sixtieth anniversary in 1985.

at the time. So, I suspect that is how they ended up with two little babies named Loretta and Bernetta. I think they found the matter of our middle names a little easier since my father had two sisters named Laura and Hannah. Ultimately, therefore, I'm Bernetta Laura and my twin is Loretta Hannah. Our older sisters soon gave us our nicknames, Bernie and Lorie.

My grandmother on my father's side thought these names were much too long for such little girls. If she'd had her way we would have been Eva and Iva. Not sure about that one. But Lorie and Bernie were sufficiently short for my grandma, and Bernie has suited me just fine ever since. Little did my grandmother know that it would be our last name that would pose the greatest challenge. No one—and, I mean, no one—could figure out how to pronounce our last name, Oebser. Until I married Everett, I would have to explain to people attempting to read it that the pronunciation of my German surname was like "Abe as in Lincoln" and "sir as in 'yes, sir!'"

It wasn't too long after we were born that our family moved to a farm nine miles east of Menomonie, Wisconsin. Just a half hour west of Eau Claire, our property was 80 acres of farmland and 40 acres of woodland.

We hadn't been there all that long when my mother gave birth to my brother, James. That was very exciting for my father. He finally had a boy. So now they had six girls and one boy.

Perhaps out of habit—but more likely just a typo—when the birth announcement appeared in the local newspaper it was declared they'd had a girl. The next week the correction ran with the headline, "OH JOY IT'S A BOY."

My grandmothers were both important to me during my childhood. Grandma Julia Stainer is shown in the inset photo with us shortly after we were christened Bernetta and Loretta. (I'm on the left.) Top: Grandma Emma Oebser (front) was always making something special for us when we were children.

Living on a farm is hard work, but it creates lasting memories—some of which I mined for my art years later. Here, Lorie, James, our dog, and I sit in the field. Our outdoor toilet, the small building in front of the larger one, can be seen. Facing page: My mother's darning basket and tools, along with two of my farm-inspired paintings.

Life on the Farm

On the 160-acre farm in Menomonie, my parents grew corn, wheat, and at times peas and beans. We raised cattle, pigs, and more than a thousand chickens, whose eggs we sold. Before my parents bought a tractor, horses were used to plow the fields. My parents also relied on the children to keep the farm operating, and I remember as a five-year-old having to get up early to chop corn or tend to the chickens before school.

Every spring there was a fairly large area that was plowed for a vegetable garden. My mother planted almost all the vegetables our family would consume and canned enough to last for the year. When we were little our home didn't have electricity so my mother washed our clothes in a Maytag wringer washer, ironed them with a flat iron, and regularly darned our clothes to extend their life. She had a foot-powered Singer throttle sewing machine that she used to sew some of our clothes. My mother was a fabulous gardener and cook—as a matter of fact, she was a very determined soul, and whatever she set out to do she did extremely well. She worked very hard and long days, and one can only image that with seven children, a working farm, and so few conveniences she was a strong woman.

My favorite memory was coming home from school and smelling the bread that my mother had just baked. She would give us a slice with butter that quickly melted into the soft, warm bread. It was the best.

Fall Scene in Wisconsin / Oil on Canvas / 30" x 30"

Peggy's Chickens / Oil on Canvas / 30" x 30"

My parents were bonded by their deep religious faith. From the time they married in 1925, facing page, they lovingly supported each other, and their faith was a great gift to us as children. Above left: Lottie and Herman in the 1960s.

Our farm's produce was mostly for our own sustenance. The exception was the field of green beans, above, which we kids picked for Durand Canning Company—keeping part of the proceeds to buy our clothes. Left: Our farmhouse, captured in the 1990s.

Honoring My Mother

When I was deciding exactly what objects were going to be used for my mother's memoir, I didn't have to search for items that could represent her. I had known for some time that I was going to use my mother's flat iron and her darning aid.

I'd chosen these items because there was something about the sewing basket where the darning aid was kept that seemed almost sacred in our home. We all knew it had a special place where it was always kept. My mother darned our socks and mended our clothes, and we knew that it was important to her that our clothes not only last as long as possible but also look presentable.

Like my father, my mother was a very strong person. I believe the challenges they went through and the way they lived their lives instilled in me the strength that has helped me survive.

My mother and father worked so hard for what they had, and they never made a secret of it. Their effort to do whatever they had to in order to be their best was a lesson to us growing up. When they were older and my mother had a stroke, my father took care of my mother until he died.

A couple years after my father passed away I went back to help with my parents' estate sale. At that time I found my mother's sewing basket with the darning aid, pincushion, scissors, and thread. I also found the flat iron. I brought all these back with me and started to decide how to assemble them into a sculpture.

As I got more involved in working out a good design for the sculpture I realized it would be much better if I had one more object to make it more interesting.

I remembered that my twin sister and her husband had found an old bottle when they were walking along one of the fields on the family farm. It was an antique soda bottle that had J.B. LUTZ MENOMONIE, WIS stamped into the glass.

I will always be grateful to them for sharing; it was just what I needed to make her piece work. The fact that it was part of the farm for all those years made it special.

Mother's memoir was created by utilizing the lost wax method. It was challenging and very gratifying after it was finished.

Mother's Memoirs / Bronze / 13" tall

In 1989 I produced a metal sculpture, left, in honor of my mother, using items that represented for me her life and work. Facing page (clockwise from left): My mother holding Lorie and me; a portrait I painted of my mother in 2005; and the objects, molds, and castings used to produce the sculpture.

Lottie Oebser / Oil on Canvas / 16" x 20"

Father's Hunting Dogs / Oil on Canvas / 12" x 16"

My father loved hunting and fishing, making a dried muskie head a perfect emblem for his memoir, facing page. Counterclockwise from top left: My father with his hunting dog; my father with a string of fish he'd caught; and the picture of hunting dogs I painted as a gift for him.

Remembering My Father

For several years I had wanted to do a special piece of art that would be a remembrance of my father. I knew I wanted to do it in bronze, but it seemed to take time and patience for it to take form. At that time I was taking a metal sculpture class at Olympic College, and knew that if I were going to do a sculpture that would best represent what was special to my father, we would need to begin the process together.

Since my parents lived in Wisconsin and we were living on Bainbridge Island, our time together was limited. This was a particular point of sadness for me, and probably the most difficult aspect of moving to Bainbridge. But knowing that, through my art, I would be able to honor my father—a man who represented a seemingly endless store of strength, hard work, and love—provided a measure of solace as I struggled with being so far away from my ailing parents. After my mother suffered a stroke in 1975, my father did everything for her. At age eighty-nine, he was still dressing, bathing, and preparing her meals all on his own.

During one of my visits with them in 1987 to celebrate Easter, I was able to get my father to agree to look in the machine shed and barn with me for objects that I could use as reference for a sculpture. It was like magic when I lifted up an old board and there was a dried head of a musky he had caught forty years earlier. I knew immediately that this was exactly what we wanted since my father loved to fish and hunt. I was ecstatic, and I knew by his expression that he was thrilled that we found something that brought back fond memories.

But what really made the piece so special was the time we spent together and the shared excitement of finding our treasurer. As it turned out, that time together was more special than I could have imagined: my father passed away in July of that year.

The strength and determination with which he faced his own passing has always stuck with me, and I will forever be grateful that he seemed to have waited until I was visiting again, this time to attend Lorie's and my high school reunion. I had just arrived at Lorie's house in Saint Paul when we received a call from my mother. She told Lorie that something was wrong with my father: he had gotten her up and dressed and fed before dawn, far earlier than he usually did, and then had gotten back in bed himself. Lorie and I rushed to Menomonie. When we got there, Lorie looked after my mother and I went to my dad. He looked horrible, and it was clear to me that the end was near. However, after we arrived, he managed to get himself up and dressed.

I told my father that I was going to call an ambulance, but he asked that I drive him to the hospital instead. I told him that I wasn't sure I could find the hospital—the years spent away from the area had made many of the roads unfamiliar to me. My father reassured me that we would find it together. And we did.

When we arrived at the hospital my father insisted on walking in under his own power. However, once he was inside, the staff quickly put him on a gurney. Lying there, my father asked me for a pen and paper so that he could write a note to my mother, and to this day my greatest regret is that I did not immediately get them for him. Not long after that, he lost consciousness and never recovered.

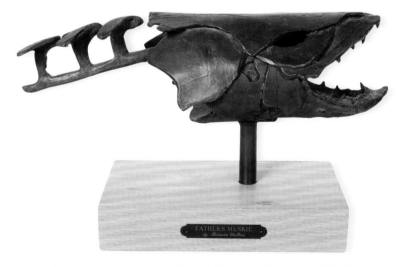

Father's Memoirs / Bronze / 11" tall

Schoolhouse

Lorie and I started grade school at the age of five. It was a two-mile walk, but it seemed more like twenty on those sub-zero days in Wisconsin. Fortunately, after two years, arrangements were made for a neighbor to transport those students who lived two or more miles from school.

We went to Beyer Settlement School, where all eight grades were taught by one teacher. There were about twenty-five students in the one-room school.

A brick structure with stairs leading up to the entrance, the schoolhouse had a large hallway flanked by two doors, one going to the library and the other to the large classroom. There was also a basement with a large open space where we could play during recess on those cold winter days.

We had a chemical toilet in the basement (the original unisex bathroom) that we considered a luxury. We drank from a large ceramic water fountain, which was fed by the well next to the school; the students took turns pumping the water.

The youngest members of our one-room schoolhouse were photographed when Lorie (far right) and I (third from right) were in the first grade, the year I started wearing glasses.

Childhood Memories

One day I was looking at some of the things I had on a shelf, and my childhood doll caught my attention. Earlier I had been thinking about doing a painting that featured objects from my childhood, and this fond relic of my past seemed the perfect subject.

The doll had special memories for me since it was a gift from my two oldest sisters, Lois and Edith. They were first-year schoolteachers when they used some of their wages to buy my eight-year-old twin sister, Lorie, and me each a doll and buggy. They were delighted to be able to buy their little twin sisters such lovely Christmas presents, and Lorie and I were thrilled to receive them.

The dolls were identical with the exception of the color of their dresses: Lorie's was pink and mine was yellow. We each gave them our favorite name, so I christened my doll "Connie" and Lorie named hers "Patsy Ann." She was one of only two dolls I had growing up. My grandmother had given us both small dolls when we were about two. Mine had gotten broken, though, so I was overjoyed to receive one so beautiful.

The pink dish I paired with my doll in the still life was a candy dish my mother would put sweets in for all special occasions. The small Valentine heart candies with all the little sayings were my favorite.

Childhood Memories / Oil on Canvas / 16" x 20"

Reflections on Bernie

by Lorie Thompson

One of my first memories of Bernie was our holding each other's hand. It made me feel so secure. On October 26, 1939, I was blessed with a beautiful soul mate, Bernie—a twin to share life's experiences.

Bernie and I were so lucky to have grown up on a farm with our five other siblings. The farm, where growing our food was paramount, taught us respect for the earth. Our mother had a green thumb. She always had a beautiful garden filled with vegetables for canning. But the flowers were so special too. We loved to pick a bouquet of these flowers and to put them everywhere in the house.

Bernie and I were always so excited for spring and summer to arrive. Two of our favorite pastimes were playing in the sand and making mud pies. Every mud pie had to be decorated with chamomile flowers and weeds. We always made sure our older siblings were available to judge our pies. Our little brother Jim and I were usually runners-up since Bernie's artistic abilities were present even then, at age five or six. So, needless to say, she got all the blue ribbons.

Oh, there was such fun playing dollhouse in the corn-crib, which was empty until harvest. We had dolls that were, at first, provided us by Grandma Oebser; later we played with the ones our dear sisters, Lois and Edith, gave us. I especially recall many years of fun and joy with our dollies, Connie and Patsy Ann. In the corncrib, we would set wooden crates all around us to furnish a fantasy world for our dollies. This was the place where we also made our mud pies and where they were judged. Whatever our play for the day, we brought along our hopes and dreams of being in some sort of never-never land while in that crib. Our childhood's beauty and innocence was in appreciating these sorts of simple pleasures.

As a family we played a lot of cards. The two games played the most were Five Hundred and Cribbage. Bernie and I would organize the Five Hundred games and give out little trinkets as prizes to the winners. We also played a lot of softball as children. There was a patch of chamomile next to the woodshed that served as our playing field. During the games we each chose a baseball player idol that resonated with us and pretended to be him. I would be remiss if I forgot our love of Annie-Annie-Over during summer in those early days. We waited with such anticipation to be so fortunate as to actually catch the treasured ball that was flung over the roof by the kids on the other side. Again—simple pleasures.

As little girls, we knew our talents were unique and different, Bernie's being artistic and mine athletic. I knew even as a youngster that Bernie was creative. When Bernie and I were ten, we joined a local 4-H club named Prairie Ramblers. We chose "Home and Yard Improvements" as part of our project. It included removing weeds and poison ivy from the front yard. This extended our yard a lot, but what we didn't anticipate was that someone would have a lot more mowing to do. During our tenure as 4-H'ers, we also painted the woodshed and machine shed. We were always so pleased with our accomplishments, as they made everything so bright and cheery. (Did I mention that the paint chosen was a bright red?)

Bernie's later injury had a profound effect on both of us. It was so difficult to see my sweet sis suffering so much. But life brought the two of us some fun times with one another too. We had fabulous vacations together, for one thing. Our train trip to visit friends in Albuquerque was great fun. On that trip, we spent a day at White Sands, New Mexico—somehow feeling like little schoolgirls again, playing in the sand as we did. The next day we went to Carlsbad Caverns. (What sticks in my mind most to this day is knowing that bats dwelled there.) We also flew to Juarez and Chihuahua, Mexico, for a few days. In Juarez, we went to a violence but impressive in its pageantry. I think our little hearts were ready to pop out of our chests.

Lorie and I were inseparable companions from childhood through our early thirties.

To me, the highlight of all our vacations taken together was our trip to Europe—the most memorable of them all. We were so fortunate to have a seasoned tour guide (in his sixties—so old!) who took us under his wing and shared lots of places with us that most people don't get to see. I found Lucerne, Switzerland, awesome and majestic—a place of beauty. To me, it rated highest of all. Mount Pilatus was awesome, though, too. Our cruise down the Rhine was perfect for a sunny afternoon. Fun and laughter abounded, and the bond of love between Bernie and me grew on this trip even more than before, and it has lasted forever.

Bernie and I bought a little pink house to live in together on Highland Parkway, in Saint Paul. We chose the location because we could be closer to nature and have a garden and pets. So we planted that garden, making plenty of room for loads of flowers.

Art has always been such an integral part of Bernie's life, from decorating mud pies to painting the woodshed to designing gardens. But her talents were really developed after her marriage to Everett. For one thing, Bernie started making hundreds of cards for family and friends over the years. Each one was unique and beautiful. Included in the cards were pictures she had taken of our family on her trips to visit us, back home. Her angel cards were always my favorite. I have never thrown away one card she gave me—each one is priceless and special. Every season I decorate the house with the cards she gave me.

To my later surprise, I discovered Bernie began making beautiful ceramic pieces. I have been a recipient of some of this work. During Halloween and Christmas our home turns into a showplace, because Bernie gave me so many pieces.

It was when Bernie arrived in Houston and was under the guidance of the sculptor Willy Wang that her creativity blossomed anew. She worked in metal sculpture. While there, among other pieces, she made a bronze statue called *Boy Holding a Cat*. My husband Skip and I have that work of art displayed in our family room.

It seems to me that art has actually developed Bernie in so many ways—spiritually, for one. And it has allowed her to express love, to grow more patient, and to convey her compassion for all humankind—qualities we all aspire to achieve.

Bernie and I are so blessed to have one another. We may be many miles apart, but I feel her loving presence many times a day. (I'm so lucky to be a twin.) She will always be my precious, beautiful, "angelic" sis.

Because of the age gap between our older sisters and ourselves, Lorie, James, and I were close playmates. Above: Lorie and me (right) at age twelve with our brother, preparing to go sledding. Right: Our third eldest sister, Irene (center), was in high school by the time Lorie (left) and I (right) entered grade school. Facing page: Lorie (right) visiting me on our parents' farm while I recovered from back surgery.

Abstract #1 / Oil on Masonite / 18" x 24"

Concrete Evidence / Oil on Masonite / 16" x 24"

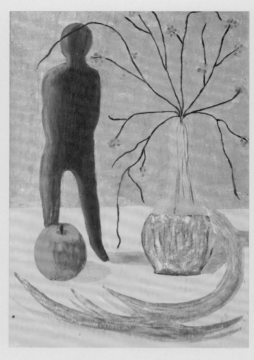

Still Life / Oil on Masonite / 16" x 23"

Red Geranium / Oil on Canvas / 24" x 20"

The earliest artwork I produced, for classes I took in college, represented a more modernist style than I would lean toward in later years. Only the flower seems reflective of my later work, though the style was less impressionistic.

Abstract Figure / Oil on Canvas / 20" x 24"

Flowers

My love for flowers goes back to my childhood. I'm not sure whether the love for flowers is a genetic trait or one my siblings and I inherited from witnessing how much our parents loved growing flowers in our garden and yard. Regardless, all my siblings love flowers as much as I do.

Flowers are one of God's creations that have brought joy to mankind since time immemorial. They satisfy our sense of touch, sight, and smell, and they have been a token of love and beauty in more ways than I could possibly imagine.

As a little girl I remember seeing this verse in my grandmother's old autograph book:

Roses are red
Violets are blue
Sugar is sweet
And so are you.

This was my first exposure to flowers being used in poetry and I remember how much I loved it.

Since I always have a small camera with me, I have been able to take many great photographs of flowers that have served me in my art. I have used the photos in card making, as references for oil paintings, and as objects of art in their own right.

Flowers have also given me the opportunity to let people know how much they are loved. I enjoy the process of finding a special vase that I think they will like and then going to the floral shop for the flowers I think they will love. It is always my hope that the recipient enjoy the flowers as much as I did during the search for the perfect gift. It makes my heart sing and brings me great joy.

Roses and Pearls / Oil on Canvas / 20" x 20"

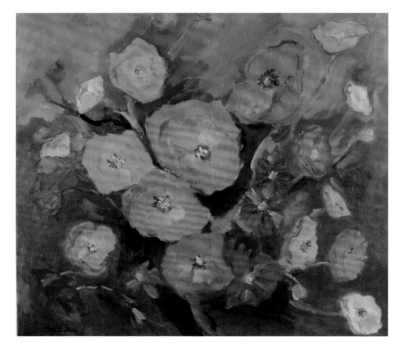

Poppies on Bainbridge Island / Oil on Masonite / 30" x 30"

...me, are among the most beautiful ...nature, and I have painted scores of ...out my lifetime. My mother, who ...s in her garden, inspired my love of ...life form. Here I stand alongside a ...er top (25" x 59") from our Lafayette ...e we had our kitchen remodeled, I ...d displayed it in my studio.

In addition to painting flowers, I love to grow and photograph them. Above: Pink roses grown in our garden on Lafayette Avenue on Bainbridge Island. Right: My grandmother's autograph book. Facing page: Some of my favorite paintings of flowers.

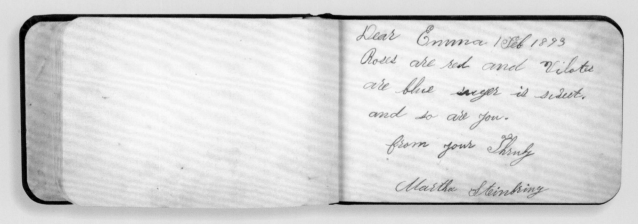

Dear Emma 1 Feb 1893
Roses are red and Vilotes
are blue sugar is sweet.
and so are you.
from your friend

Martha Steinbring

Garden on Lafayette #1 / Oil on Canvas / 16" x 16"

Garden on Lafayette #2 / Oil on Canvas / 16" x 16"

Floral Abstract / Oil on Canvas / 24" x 24"

Roses and Wine / Oil on Masonite / 25" x 24"

PHOTOGRAPHY

—

When I was in my teens I remember taking pictures of the family with a camera my sister Edith brought home with her. That was all it took to make me want one of my own. Because she knew how much I immediately grew to love taking pictures, she gave me hers and bought a new one for herself.

This was the mid-1950s when they had box cameras. The box Kodak cameras, like all cameras until digital ones became ubiquitous in the mid-2000s, had rolls of film you bought separately and put into the device. Afterward, you would drop off the completed roll to be developed, and then pick it up on your next trip to the drug store.

Photography has been important to me in that it's served me in many ways in assisting with the completion of my art—just as it has also helped me flesh out what's been important in my life experiences. Back in the days of my youth, when you mentioned "art," it was painting that was the usual medium people thought of. People back then didn't think of photography as art. Not at all. For 180 years, people have doubted this, asking: Is photography art?

At an early meeting of the Royal Photographic Society in London, which was established in 1853, one if the members complained that photography—"the new

My travels with Everett have allowed me to engage in a more mobile form of my art, photography. Here, a profile of the Colosseum in Rome, Italy.

In addition to visiting some amazing sites around the world, the Pacific Northwest has provided ample inspiration for my photography. This page (clockwise from top left): The Eiffel Tower; New York City's Times Square; inside the Colosseum; and Cape Town, South Africa, with Table Mountain in the background. Facing page (clockwise from top): Seattle's waterfront; the view of the Point Monroe Sandspit from our home on Lafayette; and a young attendee of the Olympic Music Festival when it was in Quilcene.

I loved capturing this detail of Raphael's Stanza della Segnatura ceiling during Everett's and my visit to Rome in 2011.

technique"—was too literal to compete with works of "art," because it wasn't able to "elevate the imagination." In the 1960s and '70s, photography as art was still being questioned. Today, photography seems to me to be just as legitimate as any artistic endeavor. But even in these tech-savvy days when more people use cameras than they ever had before in history, my research indicates that the question as old as photography itself—whether "the new technique" is an art—still surfaces.

Some years ago, however, I noticed that the traditionalists had seemed to have lost some pretty significant ground in their position as to photography as art. Photographs had found their niches within some of the world's major art institutions, such as New York Museum of Modern Art and London's Tate.

Ansel Adams, photographer of fabulous landscapes, has been quoted as saying, "You don't make a photograph just with a camera. You bring to the act of photography all the pictures you have seen, the books you have read, the music you have heard, the people you have loved." Truthfully, I must admit that I had never thought of it that way, but it resonates with me. As for my personal use and opinion about photography, there are many times when I have considered my own photographs as pieces of art in their own right. Like other expressions, I judge each photograph on its own and by the quality of its color, composition, ability to visually excite, and success in "saying" what I want it to say.

Of course, I have taken thousands of photographs over time and used them in as many ways as one might imagine. For one thing, like so many others might do, I have many wonderful photo albums filled with memories I continue to review and cherish. The memories I have of taking family photos are precious. Whenever we had any family gatherings I was usually the only one who arrived with a camera. When I would announce that I wanted to take their picture, my sisters would usually grumble, "Now we have to go comb our hair and put on lipstick." It took a while, but most of the time I got great photos that I will cherish the rest of my life.

Beyond refreshing memories, though, I use countless of my photos as reference material for my drawings, oil paintings, and sculptures. I remember having taken pictures of my two nephews when I was visiting them in Wisconsin and then using those photos to assist me in a sculpture that depicted the two of them. For the process of sculpting, it was necessary to take many, many photos from all angles since the boys were of course not able to pose for me in person. The photographs were invaluable to me back in the studio.

Sometimes, other photographers' work serves as inspiration or reference material for my paintings. A few of my favorite pieces were inspired by a photograph an art teacher gave the class to reproduce on the canvas.

The camera has also allowed me to capture some fun subjects to paint. When Everett and I were in Shanghai, we discovered a new Starbucks coffee shop that had just been built there—the first in that region. It was a charming setting, and I photographed it. When we got back from our trip it was one of the first paintings I did from the many taken on that trip and, naturally, I used my photo as a reference. A short time later I was surprised and very much tickled that some photographer from the *Wall Street Journal* had taken an almost identical photograph of that same Starbucks installation—from the same distance away from its façade and at the very same angle. There was "my picture" in the newspaper, big as life and looking just like my recently completed oil painting.

Everett and I keep up with our many friends across the country through Christmas letters—penned with humor by Everett—and special occasion cards made by me.

Seattle Street Scene / Oil on Canvas / 14" x 18"

Sometimes I love a photograph so much that it inspires me to paint the scene, usually with a few minor alterations—my artistic license! Here, I made the Great Wheel a bit more prominent in the view down Seattle's Union Street.

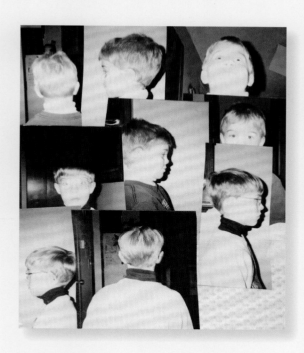

Marilyn's Aunt / Oil on Masonite / 11" x 19"

Photographs are often necessary reference material for the art I produce. Top right: I put my nephews through a complete survey of their craniums before I attempted to reproduce them in clay, top left. Above: Archival photographs, like this one I spotted in the guest bathroom of our friends Doc and Marilyn Abbott, have served as reference materials as well.

When I encountered the new Starbucks in Shanghai, I was moved to photograph and then paint it from what I thought to be its most evocative angle. Apparently I was not alone, as nearly the exact same shot was captured by a *Wall Street Journal* photographer.

THE WALL STREET JOURNAL.

TRAVEL

Shanghai Chic

STARBUCKS COFFEE

上海豆商店

Shanghai Nights

Here's a sampling of high-end hotels in Shanghai.

HOTEL/WEBSITE	RATES	COMMENTS
Four Seasons fourseasons.com/shanghai/	$300 to $6,039	Opened in February 2002, this hotel is on the itineraries of luxury tour groups like Abercrombie & Kent. Fitness center has yoga, Tai Chi.
JW Marriott marriott.com	$200 to $470	Four-month old hotel has a discreet entrance, small ground-floor lobby. Guests say location and 38th-floor restaurant help make up for it.
Portman **Ritz-Carlton** ritzcarlton.com/hotels/shanghai	$190 to $4,500	One guest says it feels like New York's Ritz-Carlton—perhaps because of a Hard Rock Café, Starbucks and Tony Roma's in the same complex.
The Peace Hotel shanghaipeacehotel.com	$160 to $1,000	It's not the most luxurious, but this Bund hotel is historic, with its famous Old Jazz Band. Noel Coward completed his play "Private Lives" here.

Twins in the Twin Cities

My twin sister Loretta, who goes by Lorie, and I lived together for almost all of our first thirty-five years. I think everyone just expected it of us, and it wasn't until I married Everett that either of us considered anything else. We lived together at our parents' farm, of course, and we both went off to two years of college after graduating from high school.

With three children in college and financing not as available as it is today, sending us to school for even two years was a sacrifice for our parents. But those two years were enough to make us employable, so in 1959 Lorie and I left home for an apartment in Saint Paul, Minnesota, the "twin city" to Minneapolis, about sixty miles due east from Menomonie.

I took a job in accounts receivable at Donaldson's, a department store where one of the most defining events of my life took place. In May of 1960 I was sitting at my desk in a rolling chair that was so tall that my feet couldn't touch the floor. (I'd asked repeatedly for a chair better suited to my 4' 11" frame, but to no avail.) When I pushed the chair back to answer the phone for someone who had gone to lunch, the wheels on the chair locked. I was too far from my desk and there was nothing else to grab hold of so I flipped over backward. The heavy chair crushed my coccyx and injured one of my vertebrae.

Lorie and I were just twenty years old at the time. I couldn't return to work, and doctor after doctor told me that I would need surgery, but the department store resisted my claim. It was not until my case was taken by attorney Gilbert Schlaegel that the store agreed to pay for my surgery and send me to vocational school. I had my surgery at Mount Sinai Hospital in Minneapolis in December of 1960 and spent most of an entire month in intensive care there.

Lorie stayed on in our Saint Paul apartment while I recovered back at our parents' farm for nearly two years. Those years were just awful. I then attended vocational school in Eau Claire. By the time I returned to Saint Paul to

work for an insurance company, Lorie had taken a room in a home owned by Helene Reed. I moved in as well.

Helene was a warm, fun lady twenty-some years older than Lorie and me. It was in Helene's home that I began to blossom as a person and discovered that life could be more than just the grind of hard work. At Helene's we would cook together, and when Helene would go home to visit her family, we would often tag along, too. Helene even visited our parents' farm with us. At Helene's we felt like we were part of one big family.

It was while living at Helene's that I decided to take my first art class as an adult, a class on painting. I felt it was something I needed to do: after our hard childhood on the farm, my excruciating injury, and my grim recovery, I felt that there had to be more to life than just work.

After Lorie and I moved into our own apartment on Grand Avenue, we continued our friendship with Helene and some of her boarders. When I was twenty-nine I took a job at Great Northern Railway, which became Burlington Northern in 1970. With this job, Lorie and I had enough money to buy a nice little house in the Highland Park neighborhood of Saint Paul.

At our Highland Park home I continued to work on my art, which expanded the beauty in my life and made my world a bigger place. Travel also broadened my horizons, and Lorie was my travel partner in the late 1960s and early 1970s. We went to Canada with our sister Edie. We traveled to Juarez, Mexico, then flew to Chihuahua. There, we had the opportunity to visit with matadors. Then, in 1971, we set out on a three-week trip to Europe. I had always dreamed of visiting Europe: I wanted to see Paris, and I wanted to view Michelangelo's *David* in Florence.

My coworkers at Burlington Northern were almost as excited about our trip as I was, and they asked me to share my itinerary so they could follow along with each day's travels. The itinerary I provided also allowed them to relay the sad news of a coworker's death: they sent a letter that reached me at one of our hotels.

Lorie and I both loved Europe's food and shopping. We had a very funny guide who took us out at night, allowing us to see a slice of European life in addition to all of the important sights. I loved Switzerland and was taken by La Grand Palace in Brussels, but my favorite was the Louvre.

In 1975 I met Everett, and we were married a year later. In my heart I hated to leave my sister, but I knew I had to. Lorie stayed in our little Highland Park home until she married Skip Thompson, whom she'd met while working at 3M, in 1980.

Lorie and I led thoroughly modern lives from the time we went off to college together until I married Everett. We purchased a home in Saint Paul's Highland Park, facing page, and went on several trips together. In Rome, we hit the town in matching black wool blend hot pants—the height of 1970s fashion. In 1994, I had myself photographed in that same outfit as a surprise birthday gift for Everett.

While we lived together in Saint Paul, Lorie and I would come back and visit our parents' farm as often as possible.

The years I spent living with Lorie launched me into adulthood, including my entry into work in finance at Burlington Northern. Here I am shown at my desk in the Saint Paul office.

I painted a portrait of my twin as a toddler in 2004, using a black-and-white photograph of her as reference and another artist's painting as inspiration for the color palette and style. Below left: Lorie with her dogs Bridget (left) and Gidget in 2012.

Lorie - Twin Sister / Oil on Masonite / 9" x 12"

Reflections on Bernie

by Helene Reed

In 1964 I bought a house on Grand Avenue in Saint Paul from a Pentecostal minister and his wife. It was quite a big house, and they had been renting rooms to several young men. They asked if I would keep the boys there, and I agreed. After a year or two, I decided to continue to rent out rooms a bit longer, this time only to women.

In 1966 Lorie Oebser moved into one of the rooms, and a short time later her sister Bernie joined her as well. They were both very outgoing: lovey-dovey with each other and everyone else, and I remember they were always giving me a hug or smooch. I'm just the opposite of that. I was about a half a foot taller than they were and about twenty years older, and they were so affectionate and exuberant that I would have to remind them to not hang off my neck when they would hug me.

Bernie and Lorie were helpful and loved to cook with me, and they became the only renters that I socialized with besides one young man from Denmark, Paul Sorensen. Paul had rented from me the year before the twins moved in. We would sometimes take day trips up to one of the lakes where my family vacationed, and one year Paul and I went down to the twins' farm for Thanksgiving. Both girls really seemed to love their family. When my own folks would have family get-togethers, a lot of times we invited Lorie and Bernie to come too, so I've got all kinds of pictures of them with my family.

After about a year, the girls moved out. We all continued to remain friends—even after Bernie met Everett and they moved to Texas and then Washington. Lorie and I would talk on the phone or we'd get together. I'd see Bernie and Everett when they'd come to town: they would stop in and see me for a couple of hours, and that happened quite a few times. In the 1990s I visited her and Everett on Bainbridge Island for about a week. She talked about her artwork as we made some small trips around the area.

We've continued to be friends, even as I near my one-hundredth birthday. In 2015, Bernie, Everett, Lorie, her husband Skip, Paul and I all got together. Bernie has always seemed to me just the same as she was when she was young: enthusiastic and friendly.

The time I spent at Helene Reed's boarding house was a formative period for me, and I have kept up with Helene throughout the years. Facing page and top left: Hand-tinted portraits of Lorie and me that I had commissioned circa 1966, the year we started living with Helene. Above: Lorie and me with Helene on a visit in the 2010s. In 2015, Lorie and I brought our husbands to visit Helene Reed and Paul Sorenson, left.

Everett's keen intellect and diligence carried
him to great success at Burlington Northern and
provided a comfortable life for the two of us.
Here, Everett pauses from his work at Burlington
Northern's Seattle office in 1990.

Everett, My Soul Mate

The best thing that has happened to me in my life is Everett.

Everett and I went on our first date on June 12, 1975— but we could have met five years earlier. On March 3, 1970, his company, Northern Pacific Railway, merged with Great Northern Railway to form Burlington Northern Railroad. For five years we both worked in finance, one floor apart, but our paths never crossed until a mutual colleague, Dick Fisher, suggested to Everett that he ask me out.

Our first date was a performance of *Arsenic and Old Lace* at the Guthrie Theater, where Everett had season tickets. I had braces on my teeth and Everett was recovering from gum surgery, and we thought our shared oral woes were just too funny. We had fun together right away. Everett has a fabulous sense of humor: it's as though he just pushes a little button and out comes a joke, always something funny and lot of it rather subtle.

In addition to appreciating his wit, I felt a soul connection with him immediately. We connected at the heart level, but we also shared a bond over the life struggles we had in common. Everett also grew up on a farm and attended a one-room rural school. At the age of eight, Everett contracted polio, which left his left arm permanently paralyzed. He overcame this challenge to earn bachelors and masters of science degrees from South Dakota State University before moving to the Twin Cities in 1968 to start his career.

Everett and I were married exactly one year after our first date, on June 12, 1976. Because of my mother's poor health following the stroke she suffered in 1975 and Everett's family being hundreds of miles away in South Dakota, we had a small wedding. Just two of my sisters, Everett's friend who served as his best man, the best man's wife, and the minister attended our ceremony at

Immanuel Lutheran Church in Saint Paul. But we didn't mind: we don't need big productions to have a great time in our life together.

Everett tells people that as soon as we said, "I do," I said, "I quit!" but in reality I continued to work for several years. However, when we were transferred to Seattle in 1981, taking care of our home became my primary responsibility. Everett has been supportive of my art, appreciating that I always took Everett into consideration and anything I did with my art came second to Everett and our home.

I made art second because life is always first, and I value my life with Everett above all else.

I feel so lucky to have met and married Everett DuBois, a witty and caring man. Above: Everett and me at my parents' fiftieth anniversary in 1975, where Everett first met my family. Left: Everett on the Seattle-Bainbridge ferry, circa 2000.

After Everett and I married in 1976, above, we began to create a life and home together. In 1978 we hosted a teenage exchange student from Finland, Antti Lievestuore, far right, at our home in Cottage Grove. It was quite the experience for two newlyweds. It earned us a letter of thanks, right, from the ambassador of Finland.

The adventures continued throughout the decades, culminating in our years in the Pacific Northwest. Clockwise from bottom left: Everett and me on the ferry to Seattle; at our home on Lafayette Avenue; and on a trip to Cannon Beach.

Angels Among Us

Angels have always had a very special place in my life. We all have a guardian angel that has been with us since birth and remains with us every minute we are here on earth. I am convinced we always benefit when we invite angels into our lives, and it is definitely our choice to accept them or ignore them.

There really hasn't been any time when I didn't remember having angels around me. The best place to start when I speak about sharing my experiences with angels and knowing they were there for me was when I was at Mount Sinai Hospital in Minneapolis for a month after having had serious back surgery. It was the most painful and stressful experience of my life. Somehow, I know God sent angels to assist me with that experience. For instance, I was blessed by having the same roommate for a month and her supportive family was wonderful to me; when I went back for checkups they had me stay with them. We remained friends for a long time. There were so many other incredibly unbelievable things that happened during this long recovery period that also confirmed my belief in angels.

It was about ten years ago that I was listening to one of our local radio stations when I heard Sue Storm, known as "The Angel Lady." She was giving people who called in the names of their guardian angels and explaining how they could assist them in their lives.

I got her phone number and called her, as I was intrigued and very curious as to which angels were patiently waiting to assist me in my life. At the time, I also learned that she had written two awesome books, *Angel First Aid: Rx for*

Miracles and *Angel First Aid: Rx for Success*. I have long had a copy of each and was delighted to recently receive a signed hardcover edition of *Angel First Aid: Remedies for Life, Love, and Prosperity*.

Sue Storm has helped thousands of people learn who their guardian angels are and how they can assist in helping them live more fulfilled lives on mental, physical, and spiritual levels. I have been blessed to have her help me on an occasion or two. It's a blessed way to receive guidance.

When our intentions are pure—to add to the love and joy of the world—angels are there to answer our prayers. They are there to protect us, guide us, and comfort us. And their light-filled assistance offers a model that we on earth can follow.

I have always loved to let people know how special they are by giving them big hugs. In my heart it's my way of letting people know they are loved and very special. It's part of who I am, and I know that it's angels that keep me wanting to continue to bring love to the world in any of the ways I can.

Divine intervention will not happen unless asked. I have said for many years that there is a high level of unemployment in the angelic world—because too many people don't ask for their help. We can ask as many angels as we want to surround us, our home, our loved ones, or whatever else is dear to us. Somehow, I am sure that the higher beings not only love being asked to help but they also want it known there's no problem too big for them to assist us with.

I've come to accept that the reason angels and archangels will not intervene in our lives unless we ask for their help is because of what I understand to be the "Law of Free Will." (Although, somehow, I feel there might be

Celestial Angel / Clay / 12" x 16"

Angels are a source of comfort and inspiration to me, and I have depicted them in many of my pieces through the years. Here, three angels grace a collage I produced in the 2000s. Facing page: A clay sculpture with bronze patina of a celestial angel.

Comforting Angels / Collage / 10" x 12"

Heavenly Harmony / Encaustic / 11" x 14"

blessings that are bestowed upon us every second. As one example, I'm very grateful for all the creative opportunities that angels help me with everyday.

Angels appear in much of my art because I believe they ask me to recognize them. And so, I do so in that very special way. Angels are included in many of my collages, encaustics, monoprints, some oil paintings and sculptures. Including them in my art has brought me great joy and helped make my life more meaningful.

I once sculpted an angel out of my imagination (or, I might more accurately say, with their guidance), and it was exciting. After it was glazed and put in the kiln, magic happened. When I took it out, the glaze had melted in a way that made it look like it was made of jade instead of clay. I was so delighted.

We are all unique and are blessed with the freedom to be and do what is the best for our soul. Throughout my life I have found that the most powerful force in life is LOVE. I believe it's my gentle, evolving relationship with my angels that helped me to arrive at and to sharpen this understanding.

exceptions to this, but this is something only they know.) I used to pray for someone by asking that they be given the ability to understand what was causing their pain. However, I learned it may not be one person's place to "interfere" in this way—that maybe it's too harsh. I was instead told to pray for someone in a different way: "Pray for the best and highest good for their soul-self." This idea resonated as true for me on a soul level.

One of the most important things for us to remember when working with angels is to always have a high level of gratitude. Gratitude is an attitude that every living soul would be best to possess. We always need to thank God for all the

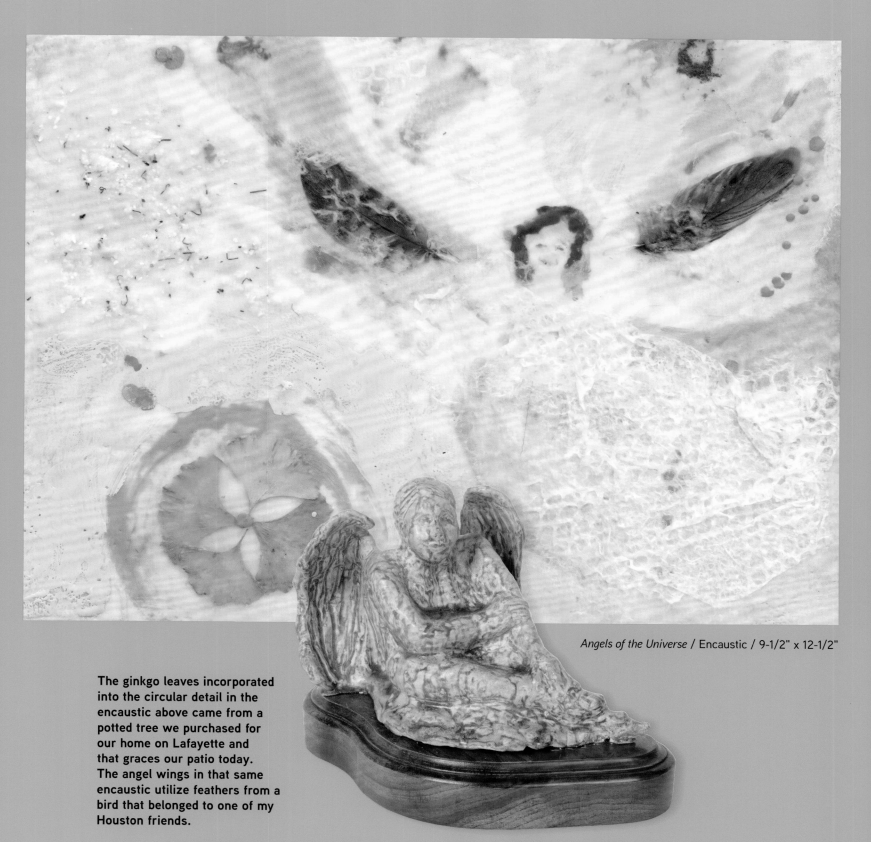

Angels of the Universe / Encaustic / 9-1/2" x 12-1/2"

The ginkgo leaves incorporated into the circular detail in the encaustic above came from a potted tree we purchased for our home on Lafayette and that graces our patio today. The angel wings in that same encaustic utilize feathers from a bird that belonged to one of my Houston friends.

Angel of Jade / Clay / 9" tall

The Adventure Begins

2

When Everett and I moved to Bainbridge Island in 1981, we had no idea what we would think of the small island community. Art classes provided an important social connection for me, shown left in the driveway of our Rhodes End Road home.

New Beginning

In November 1980, with Everett secure and happy with his job at Burlington Northern and I becoming more confident in real estate, we decided to buy a home in Woodbury, Minnesota, about ten miles outside of Saint Paul. The Woodbury house was a beautiful home on five acres, and we thought we could live there forever. However, forever turned out to be nine months.

In August 1981 we were transferred to Seattle. The prospect of moving so far away from Minnesota and Wisconsin was initially traumatic: my parents were older and I would be the first of my family to have moved any distance away. But together, Everett and I embraced the change.

Although the Burlington Northern office was in downtown Seattle, that is not where we made our home. Instead, we landed a ferry-ride away on an island about the size of Manhattan but with a fraction of the population. Why Bainbridge? In 1957, when Everett was thirteen, he came with his parents to visit a friend of his mother's on Bainbridge Island. Everett never forgot the rural waterfront community, and I agreed the idyllic island would be a nicer transition from Woodbury than the hustle-bustle of Seattle.

When we moved to our new home on Bainbridge Island it was an extremely different environment. Having grown up on a farm surrounded by corn fields, finding myself surrounded by water was a major adjustment.

Everyone has the preconceived idea that it rains all the time in Washington. It's true that the conifers make the Pacific Northwest appear lush and green year round, and we wouldn't trade this area's mild seasons for anywhere else in the world. However, when the moving van arrived at our home it was 99 degrees. We thought we had moved into a sauna. Soon Bainbridge Island returned to its comfortable late-summer temperatures and "forever" began anew.

I moved to Bainbridge Island not knowing anyone. Our house on Rhodes End in the Crystal Springs area was beautiful but, compared to life in Saint Paul, it was like living in the country. It was a bit isolating and lacked the vibrancy of city life I'd grown accustomed to. It was a really challenging time because my own family was going through difficulties as my parents aged, and the most direct route to social connections on Bainbridge seemed to be through the activities of school-aged children, which Everett and I simply did not have.

I decided to look for something to do. One day I was shopping in Winslow and saw a flyer with big letters that read "Watercolor classes taught by Charles Hill." I decided this would be a great way to meet other artists and get me back to doing something artistic. It proved to be a fun and educational class. I met Jan Herren and Mary Tate, who were the other two ladies taking the class, and our friendship has lasted all these years.

Eventually Charles moved to Oregon, but his art has not been forgotten on Bainbridge. He had done some wonderful

watercolor paintings of many of
the historical homes on the island,
some of which are on display at the
Bainbridge Island Historical Museum.

After Charles moved, I was
soon hoping to find another similar
situation where I could be creative
alongside a group of fellow artists. Fortunately,
I spotted an ad in the *Bainbridge Review* for a ceramics studio
and decided to give it a try. Karen Wilson, who ran the studio
out of her home, sold greenware pots and figurines, as well
as the paint used to decorate them, and had a kiln in her
basement. There, I worked on Santas and angels—sometimes
doing three sets at a time in a little assembly line fashion—and
Karen would then fire them in her kiln.

Painting ceramics was an enjoyable hobby that
provided the camaraderie I was seeking. I would chat with
Karen and the others who were painting in her studio. It was
a great way to meet people on the island. I kept some of the
finished pieces and sent others to friends and family. Everett
used to joke that I'd sent off so many gifts that the packages
started coming back to the house marked "no longer at this
address."

In 1984 I decided to branch out with my art by taking
classes at Seward Park in Seattle. The area was a bit dicey,

though, so I investigated classes on
the Kitsap Penninsula and discovered
Olympic College in Bremerton, thirty-
five miles away. At first I wasn't sure
it was worth it to travel that far every
day, but Everett encouraged me to go
for it. At the college I took classes on oil
painting and clay sculpture, but Olympic
College also offered a class in metal sculpture, which was
something I'd wanted to do for a long time.

The class was a lot of hard work: the process was
beyond anything I'd done before. But I was determined, and I
was really thrilled with some of the things I made. And, in the
end, I had the satisfaction of meeting a challenge I'd created
for myself.

**Shortly after we purchased our home on Fawn Trail
Circle in Woodbury, Minnesota, above inset, Everett
was transferred to Seattle. We decided to look for
homes on Bainbridge Island, where Everett had
visited with his parents by ferry in 1957, above left.
The home we bought on Rhodes End, above right,
was one of just a handful on the market at the time,
but it stunningly similar in style to the Fawn Trail
home we were so sad to leave.**

Dutch Boy / Chalk Figurines / 8" tall

Dutch Girl / Chalk Figurines / 8" tall

Balloon People #1 / Chalk Figurines / 8" tall

Balloon People #2 / Chalk Figurines / 8" tall

Although I don't consider ceramics an original art form in the same vein as painting or sculpture, it was a wonderful creative—and social—outlet for me when I took classes with Karen Wilson in the 1980s. Left: Two sets of figurines I produced in Karen's class. The Dutch boy and girl were given to Everett's mother for Christmas, and the baloon people were a gift for my parents. They all cherished them for years. Above: Everett's mother, Edith DuBois, with a Santa and Mrs. Claus I sent her. I set up a veritable assembly line to produce set after set of this Christmas couple to give to family and friends. Facing page: A set of ducks made for my father.

Pair of Ducks / Chalk Figurines / 10" tall

Reflections on Bernie

by Karen Wilson

I met Bernie when she came to my ceramics studio in the early 1980s. Sometimes she stayed for the classes I offered, and sometimes she just picked out her greenware pieces and worked at home. Although she had done art in other mediums, she was just getting into the ceramics world.

Bernie made an immediate and lasting impression on me. I remember her coming in one day and being so bubbly and interested and excited about doing things. She just jumped right in. I remember her enthusiasm—it was always infectious. Everybody knew her and was happy to see her. She was warm and friendly with everybody.

In addition to her personality, Bernie's skill struck me as well. Her finished work was always very, very good. It was meticulously done. And I think she always had a flair for expressing herself and putting what was in her mind into what she was working on.

After working for a time on ceramics, she began to get quite heavily into sculpting and painting. She was so open to try new things. I can remember discussing it with her—what she was doing and the variety of lessons she was taking. From time to time I'd see some of her work at her house or she'd bring it by my shop. I think it's amazing how she has developed and tried so many different things. When she would show me her work, she would usually discuss the idea she had for the work and whether she had trouble in developing

it or it just came to her and she was able to complete it quite easily. I remember one piece that she had with a carriage and how she described her struggle with one of the horse's feet.

Bernie and I became friends right from the start because of the type of person that she is—her vivaciousness. It's been thirty-five years now that we've been friends. Generally we go to one another's homes for dinner or to plays or things like that. One of the commonalities we have is that I am an Iowa farm girl and Everett and Bernie grew up on farms in South Dakota and Wisconsin. When you grow up on a farm, there's work to do and you do it. And I think that determination and that work ethic carry through to other things in your life. As far as her body of work, Bernie has of course expanded her range in the art world. But I don't think Bernie is capable of changing who she is—it's born in her to be warm and friendly and excited about life and people.

Of course, she has suffered so much physically that would make the average person not able to go on like Bernie does. But she really makes the best of things, handles it, and rises above it. She keeps going with enthusiasm for life and keeps up her spirit by always seeing the positive. She is pretty remarkable that way.

METAL SCULPTURE

In all my art experience, the most physically challenging for me was metal sculpture. What made it so challenging was not only the learning curve of mastering the various techniques—there was so much more involved compared to other mediums—but also the actual physical labor required by the process. I'm glad that I did it in the mid-1980s, when I was in my forties, and not now.

At the time I had no idea that these creations would be with me for the rest of my life. I also had no idea how incredibly special the work would be for my growth. There were times that things came up that made me truly believe this was the best therapy on the planet.

Sometimes we have something inside of us that needs to be challenged, so we can have an internal feeling of accomplishment. At the time, it seemed as though I was being driven by the love for the medium. For me, there is nothing more beautiful than a piece of bronze sculpture.

As I look back, it was one of the most rewarding art experiences of my life. Knowing that my body could handle this challenge—from the long drive out to Bremerton for classes to the physicality of pouring molten metal, hacking and filing at the rough piece, and maneuvering the heavy sculpture—gave me a confidence I have carried through my art for the next three decades.

My work in metal is some of my most treasured, whether it be for the pleasing finish of clay pieces that have been bronzed, or the hands-on process of casting metal sculpture myself.

Woman Combing Her Hair / Bronze / 10" x 14"

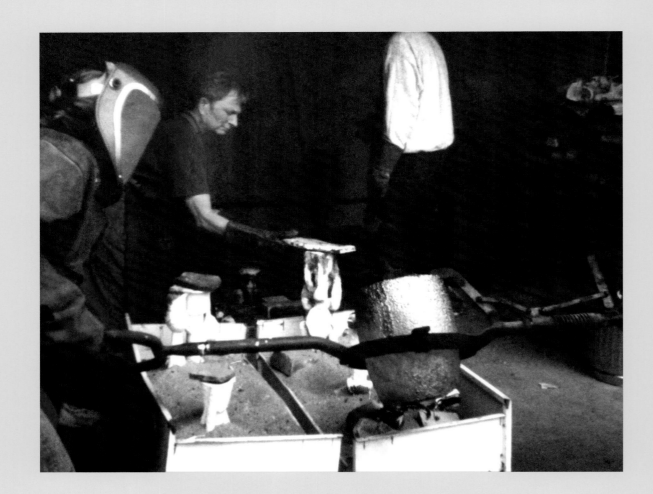

Both at Olympic College and later, at the Glassell School of Art in Houston, I threw myself into the very physical process of metal sculpture. Here, I take part in the process of casting one of my pieces in molten metal at Glassell. Facing page: My very first casting, of a Coca-Cola bottle, done at Olympic College.

My First Casting / Bronze / 9-1/2"

At Glassell I produced a playful series of sandals, glasses, and hat. Although I was not as fond of the results that came from the variation of the lost wax method practiced at Glassell, I loved how the ladylike subject matter contrasted with the heavy, industrial-feel metal.

Mermaid / Bronze / 6" tall

First Figure / Bronze / 6" tall

Royal Raspberry / Bronze / 7" tall

Woman / Bronze / 17" tall

Although the effect of cast metal sculpture (evidenced in the cat at left) is somewhat similar to that bronzed clay sculpture (all other pieces on the facing page), the process is very different. I appreciate my cast metal pieces for the hands-on role in creating them, from concept to finished piece; bronzing is best done in an outside studio. Right: A figure cast in aluminum.

Abstract Figure / Aluminum / 14" tall

One of our favorite destinations is right in our own "backyard": Hurricane Ridge in nearby Olympic National Park.

See North America First

Everett and I both grew up in the rural Midwest in an era when travel to "exotic" places was not a reality—a dream vacation was an auto trip to the Black Hills of South Dakota or to the Wisconsin Dells. And believe me, this was indeed our thinking in the early years. But how wonderfully things turned out! Looking back, I see what great fortune it was that Everett found success in his hard work. The job involved regular business travel and attendance at conventions that often allowed me to join him.

Everett and I took advantage of all those travel opportunities when we could. On or after those trips, we'd sometimes go off to other intriguing, nearby spots. And that meant that, over the course of Everett's career, we saw many of North America's historic, arty, and picturesque destinations. It was probably because my upbringing had me accustomed to a much simpler life that these many trips taken in my adulthood delighted me so.

Everett's Burlington Northern conventions took us to many fun spots like the Greenbrier in West Virginia, Boca Raton Resort and Club in Florida, the Broadmoor in Colorado, and the Biltmore in Arizona. Then, during the years Everett was working with Burlington Resources, that company's annual management meeting was at the La Quinta Resort in Palm Springs, where famous speakers, like vice president Dick Cheney; football player, coach, and analyst Lou Holtz; astronaut Jim Lovell; humor writer Dave Barry; and economic journalist Stuart Varney, all headlined.

In 1991, we attended a marvelous company-related event in Kentucky. One of Everett's business associates and friends was a lifetime Louisville resident. He invited us to attend the pageantry that is the Kentucky Derby—with seats on the finish line, no less! The day before the Derby, we saw the Kentucky Oaks (a race of three-year-old thoroughbred fillies). The stately horses were magnificent to see. Colorful hats abounded at the Derby, just like I'd always heard they would. We even sampled mint juleps. (I didn't let on that the julep didn't entirely enchant me. Such a comment in that setting might have edged close to blasphemy.) It was a fabulous trip.

My favorite trips were those taken to New York, because, for one thing, I loved that city's marvelous museums—my favorite being the more intimate collection of art to be seen at the Frick Collection. I also grew to adore the offerings on Broadway. Our first Broadway show together was in 1983, a musical called *My One and Only* that starred Tommy Tune and—conjure up the stick-figure from the fringe lands of your memory banks—Twiggy. Over the years of getting to see many Broadway performances, Everett's favorite was James Earl Jones in August Wilson's *Fences* and mine was *Cats*, which I saw three times, once in London and twice in New York. Of course, on some of those NYC trips, we saw the usual wonderful tourist attractions too, such as the Statue of Liberty, Ellis Island, the Empire State Building, and the most famous of all kick-lines: the Rockettes at Radio City Music Hall. Great stuff. We also, one time, struck out and visited West Point and FDR's residence in Hyde Park. NYC has an energy all its own.

I didn't always get to go along on Everett's trips. I recall one time he'd gone to the "Big Apple" and stayed at The Carlyle hotel (in a company apartment—employee were sometimes allowed to stay there). I later understood that The Carlyle was frequented by some pretty well-known folk. Once Everett came home from NYC after staying in those plush digs, and I asked him if anything exciting had happened. He said, "Well, as I was stepping into the elevator yesterday, Mick Jagger got on too and rode up with me." I think I let Everett down a bit when I asked (without thinking): "Does he work at Burlington Northern too?"

San Francisco was another business destination for us. What a wonderful place! I almost immediately loved the sight of its streetcars, Alcatraz, Lombard Street, the Golden Gate Bridge, and Fisherman's Wharf. And we both enjoyed hopping into a car and traveling down 17-Mile Drive, a coastline-hugging scenic road through Pebble Beach and Pacific Grove on the Monterey Peninsula. Napa Valley, with its many wineries, was also a lovely draw. It was in California where we took our first (and only) glider plane ride—a surprisingly peaceful flight, really. I wasn't in the least bit white-knuckled. I don't know why. No engine noise?

During our marriage Everett and I have lived in or near three fine cities: Minneapolis/Saint Paul, Seattle, and Houston. These places being what they were, we didn't need to travel far to find great nearby destinations—like major sporting events for Everett to attend (and me to pretend to be interested in) and zoological, art, and theater facilities for the both of us to enjoy.

Around Minneapolis/Saint Paul, for instance, was the Guthrie Theater and Walker Art Center. In 1975 we were among the first audiences to see Garrison Keillor's *A Prairie Home Companion* live radio show. It was also while living in Minneapolis that we took a few trips to the east coast where we were intrigued by the history of Williamsburg, Jamestown, and Yorktown; saw Jefferson's Monticello and Washington's Mount Vernon; marveled at the fine architecture throughout all of Washington D.C.; and lingered at my favorites, the Vietnam Veterans Memorial and the National Air and Space Museum. That same trip had us then pushing on to the Civil War battlefield at Gettysburg, Pennsylvania. The National Park Service's Rent-a-Ranger program provided a ranger to drive our own car through the military park and to give a narration of events as they'd unfolded so long ago. It was a somber experience for me, as I fully realized that Gettysburg was one of those battles where brothers sometimes killed brothers.

Seattle offered us a whole new menu of adventures. We spent time on the Olympic Peninsula enjoying the rain forests and Hurricane Ridge. We drove up to and then stayed at the rustic Paradise Inn upon the south slope of Mount Rainer. We also made weekend trips down the Oregon Coast. Cannon Beach was our favorite. From Seattle, we also hopped a flight to Hawaii and, once there, experienced our first earthquake (a 4.0)!

But for art, culture, theater, sports, and restaurants, Houston was the best. The place not only gave a big boost to my art career due to new contacts and friends made, but it was there that Everett and I further developed our growing infatuation with ballet, theater, and the occasional opera.

Houston became our gateway for many road trips to Austin, with the state capitol and the Lyndon Baines Johnson Library, as well as drives through Texas's famed fields of bluebonnets. We came to think of San Antonio as a study in diversity. We visited the Alamo and sauntered down the River Walk. Everett sampled and then announced that he highly approved of Tex-Mex food. While living in Texas, we also made a couple visits to New Orleans; struck out to visit friends in Phoenix; and traveled to the Grand Canyon, with a stop in the artsy town of Jerome. At the Grand Canyon we took a plane ride in a single-engine Cessna down into the canyon. Great fun, really—though a bit on the hair-raising side. (My knuckles were approaching a whitish shade.)

Also, while we lived in Houston, we made trips to Santa Fe and Taos, New Mexico, to gawk at the organic adobe structures everywhere you turned, the aesthetics of which satisfies something unexplainable and visceral in me. We were able to attend the famous outdoor Santa Fe Opera. We also immersed ourselves in the superb quality of the art in the shops. We bought a ballerina oil painting there and love it to this day.

Also while we still lived in Houston, I joined Everett on business trips to upscale Bermuda with its warm, sun-soaked beaches. Since Texas had us so close to the border, we also satisfied our curiosity about Mexico. We made it down to Cancún for a week. The highlights there were a trip to an ancient Mayan fortress in Tulum and a tour to another massively impressive and mysterious site of Mayan ruins, Chichén Itzá.

When late 1999 found us again Seattle bound, we turned our travel thoughts to exciting international destinations.

So the same Bernie who patted mud into cupcakes, who attended a one-room schoolhouse, and who then came home after class to her needful duties on the farm saw, as an adult, the highlights of North America that she'd only ever read about. If I think too hard on the broad arc of it, I begin to worry if I told Everett enough times how much I appreciated all that he had helped us accomplish together. Surely I did—didn't I? Of course, I did, over and over. But then . . . did he really hear it?

Our travels around the continent allowed us to see some iconic sites. Clockwise from top left: We have donned sombreros in Cancún, Mexico; flown in a glider in Calistoga, California; visited the Museum of Modern Art in New York City; and relaxed in Martha's Vineyard. Inset: Everett and me with a hula dancer at a luau in Hawaii.

Everett and I attended the Kentucky Derby in 1991 as a guest of Everett's business associate Vernon Hodge. Although I was not the greatest fan of the overly sweet mint juleps, I loved being among the pomp and fanfare, and I was excited to catch a "photo finish" with my camera, left.

Unexpected Excitement

In 1993, Burlington Resources transferred Everett to Houston and, once again, I found myself in a new place where we didn't know anyone. So, once again, I turned to art classes to form the connections I was seeking.

I joined the Art League of Houston and took drawing classes from Charles Brown at the Houston School of Art and Design. In Saint Paul I had tried thrown pottery but found my arms and legs were too short to work at the potter's wheel. Therefore, I turned my attention to hand-formed pottery and sculpting, and I was really eager to take a sculpting class. Through the Art League I learned about a workshop offered by renowned sculptor Wei Li "Willy" Wang.

Willy Wang had been commissioned to do bronze sculptures of prominent individuals from Cary Grant to George Bush, and his work was routinely sold at auction throughout the world. Willy was quite a character. He was tall, with curly hair and dark glasses. Willy had moved to the United States from China in 1981, and he developed quite a following, especially with Chinese American women in the Houston area. One of them, Heather Hwang, became great friends, along with Marilyn Woodruff and Leng Garcia. We would attend Willy's workshop and then go out for noodles in Houston's Chinatown afterward.

What I liked best about these friends was that they had the mentality of getting things done. We all had the same belief systems, we all were ambitious, and we worked. When we said we were going to do something, we did it.

One of our fellow classmates, Mike Kirby, had gone to school in Mexico City. As a favor to us, he would take our sculptures to be bronzed in Mexico, where it was far cheaper to do so. He would hand-carry these somewhat large and cumbersome pieces on the bus back to Mexico City. It was just so wonderful of him. We would have showings of our work around Houston, at places like the St. Luke's United Methodist Church or the Jung Center.

I also took some sculpting lessons from Eric Kaposta, who then connected me to Ed Hankey, an accomplished sculptor who ended up becoming a lifelong friend. I spent a lot of time with Ed. We'd work together, play together—he became almost like a brother to me. He, Everett, and I were the greatest friends, and we did so many things together while we lived in Houston.

Ed is probably the person I've learned the most from— the one who has truly done the most for me. And we didn't really approach the relationship as an instructor and student. I would just go to his studio and work on one of my pieces— sometimes there would be a friend like Cookie Joe or even a young person from Ed's neighborhood working there as well— and Ed would be busy with his own various projects. Every once in a while Ed would stop and look at my piece, giving me advice about a head that looked too small or ears that looked too big. I learned so much from Ed.

The six years Everett and I lived in Houston were perhaps our favorite. Everett is fond of saying that Houston is like a Midwest city on steroids: the same friendly nature we were used to from Minnesota and South Dakota but ratcheted up to an exciting level. We lived in a beautiful house, above and below left, and made wonderfully fun friends. Willy Wang, facing page, was among the group of artists I came to know. When we left Houston upon Everett's retirement, John and Jes Hagle, our friends from Burlington Northern, threw us a going-away party, below right.

The participants in Willy Wang's drawing and sculpture classes became more than just fellow students: many of them became fond friends.

Reflections on Bernie

by Marilyn Woodruff

You always look forward to a happy day when you are with Bernie. She's a real delight. If you want to be uplifted, she's a wonderful person to be around.

I met Bernie in Willy Wang's workshop. The first time I ever saw her in class she had these chandelier earrings on with a lot of color in them, and I was attracted to that. I also liked that she was always very friendly to everyone and shared her enthusiasm for whatever she was doing with the other members of the class. Soon, Bernie and I were friends, and after our two-hour class we would go out to lunch with our friend Leng and sometimes take a trip to Chinatown.

We had waited until we were little old ladies to take sculpting. In order to take Willy's workshop you really had to be fairly advanced in art: you weren't accepted unless you had taken art before. Many of us just wanted to perform for Willy and make him happy—I guess because we were happy to be in Willy's class. But Bernie would always keep working on it until she had something that satisfied her.

We also took a Saturday workshop that focused on painting. Bernie was great at color and would blend colors together that other people wouldn't even think of. But it made her pictures just beautiful: they were restful and just very pretty to look at.

Apart from our art classes together, I really admired Bernie for all that she put into her home and felt like I learned a lot about health just by associating with her. She was always really good at taking care of Everett: they ate well, used alternative medicine, and drank wheatgrass and water that Bernie distilled herself. Both Everett and Bernie just loved cats, and theirs were the best-treated cats I have ever seen. I remember Bernie telling me that she would put their blankets in the dryer at night so they would be warm when the cats got into bed with them. But that's how Bernie and Everett were. My late husband and I were impressed with their goodness.

Leng and I were upset when we learned Bernie was leaving Houston for Bainbridge Island and wondered when we would ever see her again. But we knew Everett was pretty active here in Houston and they traveled quite a bit, so we hoped they'd be back often. They have—I visited with them a year and a half ago when they were in Houston—and we've also kept up over the years with phone calls and cards. She continues to be just so positive and, as I've said, just a delight.

CLAY SCULPTURE

—

Sculpting in clay gives me an opportunity to work with my hands. The feel of the clay is part of what makes it special. It reminds me of my childhood when we made mud pies, bread, and cupcakes in a play area in an old corncrib. It was so much fun decorating them with the wildflowers that grew all around us on the farm.

As an adult (reluctantly putting the making of mud pies in my past), I learned how to find the clay most compatible for each sculpting project, for clay is highly versatile. In sculpture, the great joy is creating something three dimensional. And even though sculpting in wax for the projects I did for metal sculpture was much more difficult than clay, there's still the same creative process behind it all. And I loved it. It's the process of transferring a seemingly intangible idea so that it lives in a tangible material.

Sculpting the human figure has always been one of my favorites. There is nothing more beautiful than the human figure. It's graceful—one of God's most beautiful creations. By the way, this is one of the reasons I love ballet (I adore Edgar Degas' *Little Dancer Aged Fourteen*). I have sculpted many ballerinas myself—most in clay, but one in bronze.

I've completed sculptures that range in subject from the human figure to cats, from angels to fish and more. I remember loving one phase I went through,

Rendering a three-dimensional image in clay supplies a hands-on enjoyment not provided by every medium I've tried. Here, I work on a female portrait from a model at the Houston Art League with Willie Wang in 1995.

Annette / Clay / 11" tall

Samantha / Clay / 7" tall

sculpting portraits entirely out of my imagination. I put my heart and soul into these. One piece had three faces blended into one sculpture. It's my *Three Faces of Eve*. For one anniversary that Everett and I were about to celebrate, I sculpted the head of a male and female connected with hearts and roses. Another of my favorites was the head of a young girl smelling roses. These and others like them brought me joy in the doing.

There are moments when sculpting gets pretty darned exciting. On the upside, it's a thrill when a finished product passes beyond your expectations. But firing a clay sculpture in the kiln can change everything and so this adds mystery to the equation. It seems to me that anything can happen to it in that kiln. If the clay isn't as dry as you think it is, it will blow up in there. I once sculpted a self-portrait—one of my favorites—and yet watching it being carefully lowered into the kiln was the last I saw of it. These things are out of your control.

Many different forms of art enchant me, but there is something that stands out about sculpting. I have met a few great sculptors in my time—some I even now count as best friends. I can only suppose that this has played some part in my love of the medium. But of course it's more than that. At its core, it's the touch—the hands physically enfolding themselves in that gentle, earthen medium. Making something symbolic, graceful, artful, or meaningful in this particular way somehow grounds me, but at the same time there I am watching and hoping for magical outcomes.

If you'd run across the little girl Bernie in the corncrib (mud clinging from fingers to elbows) and you asked how she felt about her newly made pies and cupcakes, she might've only given you a smile or a giggle. But I know something she doesn't yet know. As part of my process when I sculpt as an adult, I feel her same fierce playfulness coursing through my veins.

Anniversary / Clay / 9" tall

Friends / Clay / 13" tall

During the years I worked with Shirley Burns after returning to Bainbridge Island, I developed a more impressionistic style of sculpture. I often chose a mottled style of glazing that gave my finished pieces the appearance of jade or ancient patina.

Heather Hwang's bright personality contributed to the joy that was Willy Wang's workshops. In addition to exhibiting together in Houston, we've kept up a fond friendship over the years.

Reflections on Bernie

by Heather Hwang

I met Bernie at the Willy Wang workshop, a sculpture class. She always came to class with a bright, smiling face, greeting everyone in this very kind, nice, warm, and soothing way. She'd call everybody "Dear" or "Darling," and to her everybody was her best friend. She's really that kind of person—very nice.

She took drawing as well as sculpture because Willy emphasized drawing as basic training to learn how to see the subject for our sculpture. We would draw from a live model, and it really improved our observation.

Bernie is a hardworking artist. She's really, really creative too. Whether it's drawing, sculpture, or collage, she always worked hard to get better, and she's still working hard. She's already a good artist but she's really persistent to get even better. I admire her dedication. After she and her husband left Houston there have been two art shows that she has shown with us. She had to make a lot of effort to mail her artwork to Houston, and she and her husband came to the exhibition's opening and reception.

Bernie is so dear to me. Every holiday—every Christmas, Valentine's Day, whatever—she creates her own cards and fills them from top to bottom, every page, with writing about her travels, her family, even her pets. She calls me as well, and we can talk for an hour about her family, her husband's family, or our old friends. Every time we have a conversation over the phone we laugh and laugh—it's really a good feeling to have a conversation with her.

Bernie's a positive person—a fun person to be with and talk to. She's also a sincere and generous person. I'm really lucky to have her as my friend.

DRAWING

———

Many different forms of art involve drawing in one way or another. In addition to traditional pen-and-ink art, painting requires underdrawing; even sculptures are often sketched out in two dimensions.

    I've never spent a lot of time drawing for pleasure, but I understand its fundamental value and have taken steps to improve my skill. My art is much more about working with my hands.

    Drawing was most enjoyable during the time I spent with Willly Wang's drawing group in Houston. I loved working with a group of friends and found I enjoyed drawing from a live model.

    I found that drawing helped me in a lot of ways, particularly in my sculpture because it prompted me to consider figures like never before.

While developing my drawing skills, I dabbled in pen and ink. The slow nature of pen and ink frustrated me: I prefer more hands-on mediums.

Trees from the Northwest / Pen and Ink / 15" x 15"

David / Pencil / 14" x 17"

Sally / Pencil / 14" x 17"

Excercise Drawings / Pencil / 17" x 14"

Claudia / Pencil / 14" x 17"

Sonja / Pencil / 14" x 17"

Willy Wang encouraged his sculpting
students to perfect their drawing.
These pages from my sketchbook
reflect the work I was doing during
this time—and later, as in the case of
the cat drawing at right.

Oscar / Pencil / 14" x 17"

Ed Hankey was a wonderful teacher as I developed my sculpting skills. In time he also became a treasured friend—and one of Everett's and my favorite people.

Reflections on Bernie

by Ed Hankey

Bernie came to work with me through Eric Kaposta, another sculptor who had given Bernie some lessons. I was doing a lot of portraits in clay at that time so that's why she wanted to take some lessons from me. It was clear she had a lot of talent and had done some stuff before I met her. Her work had been mostly impressionistic to some degree, and she wanted to get more into realism.

The first thing she worked on in my studio was a portrait of her husband. She's very determined, and when she would get an idea in her head she'd carry it through and get it completed. She didn't seem to struggle too much; she would just do her work and always seemed really happy with the results. But when the portrait of her husband blew up in the kiln after we fired it, she felt like it was a lost cause. I told her, "No, we can put back together." So she worked on it and we got it all back together. It turned out pretty well, and she felt good about her work.

And that's just the way it was with Bernie. Her attitude was always really positive, and I never found her to be a difficult person to be around. Bernie's kind of a unique individual, definitely different than most. She was much easier to get to know than a lot of people are: more open, welcoming, and warm. Her personality was really bubbly and she was a lot of fun to be around, always joking. She's just a happy, joyful type of person.

She loves looking at other artwork and studying with various people, gaining knowledge and picking up new ideas by learning from other people. She's devoted a lot of time to classes, and she's very committed. All she seemed to like to talk about, all she wanted to do, was art—to create something. She would jump around from painting to sculpting and then to ceramics for a period of time and then back into painting. It seems to me that Bernie feels a strong connection to the subject matter in her art, whether it is a dancer or something from pictures she took when she went to Africa.

Bernie's art is definitely a hobby, but it could be more if she wanted it to. Some of her latest stuff is really up there, and I'd compare it to Monet: a little bit impressionistic but just really quality-looking stuff. In the beginning she was just doing it to do it, and then she would either keep her pieces or give them away. I used to prod her about it, saying, "Man, Bernie, you need to start getting stuff up and doing a show and selling this stuff." But she said she just wanted to make the art. Finally she started showing some works and getting out there, though she's still not that interested in really trying to make a lot of money or market herself. If she was to get her stuff in New York or someplace like that I think she'd really start to have some real success, but I think her heart is more in just the joy of doing it. But the quality is still really good.

Through working with Bernie I've also gotten to know her husband. Everett is a really neat person too, with a great personality. He has a dry sense of humor and is easy going— just a wonderful person. In Houston we were always going out to dinner, or they'd invite me to a program, or we'd do some fun stuff like going to antique shows. I really enjoyed doing stuff with them. At the time, Everett wouldn't really express himself that much about Bernie's art but I knew he really liked what she did and was supportive of her work. He enjoys everything that she does and is very positive about it.

I got the chance to visit Bernie and Everett on Bainbridge Island and see Bernie's old home studio, where I helped her set up a kiln. It was very organized: her projects were all nicely filed away in different drawers, and it was certainly a great atmosphere with a nice view. It was a wonderful place to be able to work on art, and I was really impressed with the space—though not surprised. She's always just been a very organized person and kept things really neat and clean. She also has great interior decorating ability. I know some artists that are just real slobs, so it's kind of nice thing to see somebody really have a fine studio and keep it up really well.

I know Bernie has a very comfortable life. She's had some problems, too, but she always seems to be a person who concentrates on the positive.

Everett / Clay / 12" tall

Playfulness / Clay / 7" tall

Danielle / Clay / 27" tall

Boy's Best Friend / Clay / 11" tall

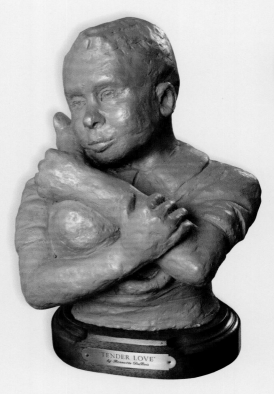

Tender Love / Clay / 13" tall

The pieces I created in Ed Hankey's studio were, for the most part, realistic, closely observed depictions of people and animals. I love capturing the human form.

Take Time to Smell the Roses / Clay / 14" tall

Edith DuBois / Oil on Canvas / 12" x 12"

Donald DuBois / Oil on Canvas / 8" x 10"

In painting portraits, I attempt to represent the spirit as well the physical features of an individual. This not only makes them recognizable, but relatable as well.

Portraits

Portraits are some of the more challenging things for me to paint. I regard myself primarily as an impressionist who paints to stimulate one's imagination. Portrait painting is just the opposite, as you want to leave nothing to the imagination. That's not to say there isn't a great deal of creativity required: what demands your heart and soul in portraiture is getting the likeness right while conveying a sense of who the subject is as a person.

Most of the portraits I've painted have been done in oil paints. I've found I can mix much better flesh colors and create more pleasing shadowing in oil. Painting from photographs has also worked well for me since getting someone to sit for you is virtually impossible.

It has been very gratifying for me to look back and see the portraits I've done for family and friends. One of my favorite portraits was also the most fraught. It was risky business, but I decided to do a portrait for Everett of his mother, whom he cherished. I loved my mother-in-law and wanted the best painting ever for Everett. This was one of those times when I knew I had help from spirit guides because the resulting painting, I feel, not only accurately captures her visage, but her sweetness of being as well.

The next most difficult subject was myself. I have no idea what possessed me, but I had the urge to create a self-portrait for my first show at Wing Point Golf & Country Club. In the process I found out that mirrors don't lie—and

Josh Roman / Oil on Canvas / 11" x 14"

Rosanne / Oil on Canvas / 24" x 30"

Child's Innocence / Oil on Canvas / 12" x 12"

neither do your fellow artists. I was very fortunate to have dear friends that I was painting with at the time whom I could ask to be brutally honest with me and critique my painting. That wasn't enough, bless their hearts: I again needed their expertise for a second self-portrait I produced for a later show at Wing Point. These were two very challenging experiences, but I'm glad I have the finished pieces.

Everett's and my first cruise
was to Alaska, for our twentieth
anniversary in 1996. In addition
to taking a daylong trip on the
narrow-gauge White Pass and
Yukon Route Railroad, near
right, we took a helicopter to
Mendenhall Glacier, below right,
giving us a close view of the
blue ice, far right.

Northern Excursion

After several years in Houston, we were lonesome for the ambiance of the Northwest and decided to do an Alaskan cruise for our twentieth anniversary. It was on Holland American and would be our first cruise experience. So in August 1996 we flew to Vancouver, B.C., to meet our ship, which would take us through the five hundred miles of the Inside Passage from Ketchikan to Juneau. The cruise portion of the trip was followed by a train/bus trip to Whitehorse, which is the capital of Canada's Yukon Territory. From there we would fly to Vancouver and then back to Houston.

After a day at sea our first cruise stop was in Ketchikan. It is a bustling town with many quaint shops and galleries. We chose to do a scenic floatplane tour in a single-engine de Havilland Otter. We made a stop by a river and a fish hatchery as the salmon were spawning and it was expected that bears would be feeding in the river. However, it was a Saturday and only one bear was working! In any event the scenery was great, and taking off and landing on the water is always exciting.

Our next port of call was Juneau, the capital of Alaska. Founded on the promise of gold in the latter part of the nineteenth century, Juneau eventually yielded immense riches before the last goldmine closed during World War II. We saw the local sights, including the Governor's Mansion and the Alaska State Museum. We also made a stop at the famous Red Dog Saloon.

This stop was followed by what both Everett and I agree was the highlight of our trip. We took a helicopter from Juneau to the Mendenhall Glacier. We landed on the glacier and did a brief trek wearing our cleated boots and carrying ice picks. The dense glacial ice is different from regular ice in that it is blue. It was a true sight to behold!

This phenomenon produced many beautiful photo opportunities. While we were there, we had the rare opportunity to see a large piece of glacial ice break from the glacier and crash into the sea.

The following morning we caught the MV *Fairweather* (a much smaller ship) for a cruise along the Lynn Canal to our evening destination of Skagway. The next day marked the last full day of the tour and had us preparing for the journey home. However, that final day was still fun as we took a trip on the narrow-gauge railroad, the White Pass and Yukon Route Railroad. It was a unique way to experience the treacherous "Trail of 98," the route followed by the hopeful souls stampeding in search of gold. We were then transferred by motor coach from Fraser, B.C., to Whitehorse for our final evening before returning home to Houston.

The trip was a good way to celebrate twenty years of marriage. Our previous thirteen years in the Northwest reminded us that you can never become jaded by beautiful scenery. We appreciated the convenience of cruising with amenities of good food, entertainment, and clean facilities, and this trip encouraged us to include cruises in our future travel plans.

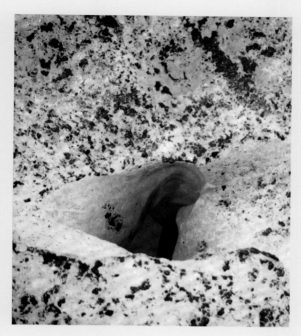

Reflections on Bernie

by Cookie Joe

One thing about me is I'm very short and I'm very perky. Well, Bernie is shorter and perkier.

I met Bernie at Ed Hankey's studio. Bernie was a student of his, and I wanted to learn to sculpt, so she and I met in his garage. We're both very energetic, very enthusiastic, and very affectionate. Ed Hankey is a quiet guy, so for him to have the two of us together in one room was a lot of energy.

Bernie decided she was going to do a self-portrait in clay. And so she did this amazing, almost life-sized piece. It was so perfect: She put hours and hours into it—her soul, really—and it looked just like her. I was so impressed I couldn't believe it. I was very jealous. And then, when it got fired in the kiln, it exploded into a million pieces. I was devastated. I mean, I cried. But Bernie had the most sunshiny attitude. She said, "That's okay, I'm just going to put it back together one piece at a time. It's no big deal." Then she started putting it back together one by one until, after a while, she lost interest and moved on. I would have been not nearly as gracious or as mature as she was about it.

The whole time she was in Houston we dined together regularly. I became friends with Everett as well. He has a wonderfully dry sense of humor, and he would make me just laugh and laugh. They were very supportive of my work and my art: they would come and see my performances, so it was a really very special relationship.

When she moved, it was very sad for me. I don't think she realizes how traumatic it was for me to see her to go. We had a great little thing going—we were artists, we were friends, and we had a nice social circle. But one thing that she left me, one of my treasured pieces and great mementos, was a brass sculpture of a ballerina she'd had in her home that I just loved.

After she moved, Bernie would come back to Houston for visits from time to time. During one of her visits, she said she wanted to gather reference material on ballerinas, so she asked if she could photograph my students. I got some ballerinas to come in, and I helped pose them. But the cool part was that she also got them in repose—just tying their shoes or resting or sitting casually. It really captured the mood of a dancer. After she had completed her paintings, she made a print of her work so the dancers could have one. It was priceless for these kids: it had been a great honor for the girls to get to be photographed and to get to see an artist's interpretation of their frame and their lines. Dancers are artists too, but our art is spontaneous and instantaneous and it only last for as long as we're in that position. For somebody to freeze that in time in her medium is a great collaboration.

Bernie has a passion for creating and expressing herself. She's not doing it for the reward of other people's opinion—the value, for her, is in the doing and her own satisfaction. The time and energy and passion she puts into her art is as serious as any professional's. It comes from her heart and I think that's what makes it so special.

And she does spread a lot of joy.

Every time she sends me a Christmas card it's handmade and I know it is full of hugs. Ours is the kind of friendship that, no matter how far or how long you are apart, you pick right back up when you get together as though you were never apart. It's that kind of friendship.

Cookie's Dance Student / Oil on Canvas / 18" x 18"

What a Pair / Oil on Canvas / 18" x 18"

Cookie Joe, facing page with a signed slipper she gave me as a going-away present, became a fun friend when I lived in Houston. On a visit back to Texas in the 2010s, Cookie let me photograph some of her dancers, providing reference material for subsequent paintings. The painting of the pointe and tap shoes above was inspired by a picture in Cookie's powder room.

As a subject, ballet utterly captures my imagination. It gives me the chance to portray the human form, and it also allows me to ponder the seemingly superhuman feats dancers manage to achieve.

Love to Dance / Oil on Canvas / 18" x 24"

Preparing for Rehearsal / Bronze / 8" x 14"

Seattle Ballet / Collage / 10" x 13"

Moral Support / Encaustic / 13" x 10"

Passionate About Ballet

Only in my wildest of dreams could I ever have become a ballerina. The best I could do was to get up on my tip-toes—that's it. I've never been able to figure out how they seem to ignore the laws of gravity as they float through the air in long, soaring leaps. How they can spin and keep in perfect balance is beyond my imagination. There are times when their feet move so rapidly that my eyes can hardly follow the movement. Then comes the amazing part for me: the fact that they are moving their bodies in perfect sync to music. No doubt, all forms of dance require practice and techniques, but I think it's safe to assume that none requires more than ballet.

The thing I love about ballet is its gracefulness. My love for the human figure and seeing the body move in a way that seems so spontaneous and effortless make it an incredibly beautiful art form to behold.

My interest in ballet came about when I was in college. Learning about Edgar Degas and all his fabulous paintings of dancers and sculptures of ballerinas left a lasting impression on me.

One of my first experiences of capturing a ballerina in my own art was when I was taking a class at Olympic College. I remember the joy I got from sculpting it in wax and then finishing the process in bronze.

Over the years I have done oil paintings, encaustics, sculptures, and collages of ballerinas. I have loved every second of doing all of them.

Above all, though, is my favorite and most beloved ballerina: Cookie Joe, who teaches ballet at the ballet school she owns in Sugarland, Texas. She became one of my closest friends in Houston after we sculpted together at Ed Hankey's, and she often invited Everett and me to attend her school's recitals. She also was so dear to have me come to her school and arrange for two of her students to dance for me so I could photograph them. I later did a couple of oil paintings that used those photographs as references.

The Ballerina / Bronze / 12" tall

Could Have Danced All Night / Bronze / 10" tall

The Grand Tour

Before leaving Houston and returning to Bainbridge Island late in 1999, we had a trip to take, for we'd already committed to a cruise from Barcelona to Istanbul on the *Grand Princess* in September of that same year. We were slated to board this ship (with its passenger capacity of 3,000—the largest cruise liner on the seas at that time) with about fourteen of our friends from Minnesota days, including our longtime good friends, Tom and Marguerite Baker.

We found that traveling with friends lived up to our great expectations, making things most enjoyably different for us in many ways. To name one, we headed out with them to dinner later at night; had Everett and I been left to our own devices, we'd have announced ourselves "done-in" and slumped peaceably to bed!

Before departing aboard the ship, we did a whirlwind (jet-lagged) tour of Barcelona, first visiting Las Ramblas, the city's legendary shopping promenade. The Barcelona high point was the long-incomplete La Sagrada Família cathedral. Those in the know informed us that the entire construction time for the "Sagrada Família" project was anticipated to last longer than that of the Egyptian pyramids. Started in 1882, the last pounded-in nail is anticipated for sometime in 2026. (That's the centennial for the architect Antoni Gaudí's death).

It was plain to see that Gaudí used the natural world for inspiration of this "most-visited" church in Spain. And we learned that, in preparation of his designs, he'd even studied and analyzed plants, animals, and geothermal formations to see how Mother Nature supports her shapes and weight. So you see, even before Everett and I and all our friends had scrambled up the cruise liner's gangplank, I was already happily vibrating about this looming, whimsical, and fantastically constructed creation.

Then we set sail for Monte Carlo, where we quickly found ourselves in surroundings well above our station. Our shopping was limited to the window variety, but still it was fun seeing high-end excesses on display. We took a short bus ride to Cannes—the home to the now-famous international film festival. It was a "nice scene" (never mind our disappointment that no one recognized us or inquired after our just-released "indie" film).

Our next port was the seaport of Livorno, near Italy's Tuscany region. It serves as a gateway to Florence—which we then toured, first viewing the magnificent bronze doors created by Ghiberti and located in front of the Duomo. Also, of course, we went to see the massive, renowned lantern dome, finished in 1436 and designed by the goldsmith and "untrained" architect, Brunelleschi. The "lantern" is the decorative marble structure crowning the dome.

As is the touristy custom for when in Florence, we lined up with countless others to get inside the Academy of Fine Arts to view its famous collection of Michelangelo statues. These included the flawless, seventeen-foot-tall David, given pride of placement standing alone in the middle of an oval, interior space, perched on a pedestal.

Florence was crowded. Very crowded. Often the charms of locations suffer from their popularity. Wondrous sights located in any town near a large cruise ship's ports get gridlocked. And, by the way, this puts a premium on restrooms. So cruise directors advised us travelers about "preferred" shops—the ones that let tourists use their facilities (in exchange for listening to a shop owner's hard sell). In Florence, in a panic, Everett and I scurried into a leather shop; upon our exit, I found myself the proud owner of a charming white leather coat. The shop owner remarked, "Now you have something to remind you of Florence." Everett turned to me and whispered, "The most expensive restroom I've ever used."

We sailed on to beautiful Naples. There, eight of us rented a van and a driver to make the trip down the Amalfi Coast. I don't think many would disagree that that drive provides the most picturesque of views in all Europe. We also stopped at Pompeii—the ancient Roman resort

In 1999, Everett and I took a European cruise with our friends from Minnesota, Tom and Marguerite Baker. From Istanbul's Blue Mosque, top left, to the Acropolis in Athens, above, the trip was filled to the brim with amazing and iconic sights.

Everett and I loved getting the chance to visit Saint Mark's Square, above right, and the canals, above left, of Venice. We also visited Florence, where we viewed Michelangelo's *David*, near left.

buried by the 79 AD eruption of Mount Vesuvius—and saw captivating artifacts from ancient times.

Then came Venice. All of our Minnesota group leaned against the railing on the edge of the cruise liner's top-most deck and smiled down as we approached the City of Canals. Some of us wondered aloud how magnificent it might be to see that historic visual delight from even higher up—from a hot air balloon. Rumors abounded about Venice's crowds, smells, and commercialism, but any concerns about those things quickly evaporated in the magic of our event-packed time there.

We saw Saint Mark's Square (its pigeons famously posing for selfies atop tourists' heads). We toured Saint Mark's Basilica. We climbed the bell tower (the Campanile di San Marco) that stands just opposite the basilica and offers a panoramic view of Venice. And we saw the Doge's Palace. Yes, we had to go on a gondola ride in the Grand Canal too. Clearly, a touristy thing but fun—and we were amazed by the skill of the gondola operator.

Another day of cruising brought us to Athens. The main attraction on our tour while there was the Acropolis, the elevated outcrop that is home to the Parthenon. In general, however, we found it best in Athens to focus on what had been and not necessarily what currently was. In hindsight, I realize there'd been clues that emerged from all around us—hints that Greece would be in economic shambles a decade later.

We moved on to Turkey, and was I ever impressed! Our first stop was Kusadasi, which lay along a coast with great pedigree. It's the region known as Ionia, and it included Ephesus and some other of the great cities of the ancient world. We toured Ephesus, discovering that it had once been a commercial center and the Roman capital of Asia Minor. Truly impressive ruins remain there; the ancient Roman engineering astounded us all, bringing about our fantasies of past grandeur. We also briefly checked out the local shops. (Not a white leather coat in sight, but I scored a very nice bracelet!)

The biggest positive surprise for me (when compared to my preconceptions) was our final stop in Istanbul. It was a most modern, clean, and friendly city. We filled our time to the brim with sightseeing. We started out, of course, with what dominates the skyline as you sail into the city: the seventeenth-century Blue Mosque, filled with more than 20,000 Iznik tiles in thirty-three shades of blue. We also toured the sixth-century Byzantine Underground Cistern that is magnificently supported by 336 marble columns. A motor coach then took us to the Topkapi Palace, an impressive, treasure-filled imperial residence.

We finished with a walk through the Grand Bazaar. Originally built in the 1450s and the largest covered market in the world, it comprises more than four thousand shops along sixty-five snaking streets. Seemingly sure-footed (as though he were a local), Everett steered me on this stroll through the colorful mobs, down winding alleyways of shops and stalls. For this I was thankful at the time, though I recall being vaguely curious why no booths we passed sold leather goods.

We, in time, retreated to our Istanbul hotel for a final toast with our travel-mates, our Midwest friends. Getting to encounter, as we did on this trip, examples of the world's most stunning art and architecture was a most marvelous thing. But any trip taken with friends is a reward in its own right. Combining the two—traveling with good friends while seeing special spots and sharing in the group's reactions—provides an enhanced liveliness. As it did for us on this trip as we all encountered together the spectacle of Antoni Gaudi's cathedral, the grandeur of Saint Mark's Square, and the breathtaking allure of Istanbul's Blue Mosque.

I'll not soon forget it.

African Safari

In 1999 we took our first major international excursion, a safari to Kenya and Tanzania called "Wings Over Migration." The trip occurred in January when huge herds of animals were migrating in search of fresh grass and water. Our tour was made up of a small group that moved from location to location via a single-engine plane. It saved considerable time and was much more comfortable than the primitive road systems. The biggest concern was that the runways were clear of giraffes and warthogs before takeoffs and landings.

It would be the first of our three trips to Africa (counting Egypt), and I consider them the most exciting travels in our life together. Since I adore animals, I was continually enraptured as each day we explored and photographed large concentrations of wildlife. I believe my photos speak to my utter elation at having witnessed such exotic scenes.

After a nighttime landing at Kilimanjaro, we went via caravan to Arusha, Tanzania. The following day we were on to the 5,600-square-mile Serengeti National Park. The Serengeti supports one of the largest concentrations of wildlife in the world. Within no time our eyes feasted on zebras, antelope, hyenas, leopards, giraffes, lions, buffalo, cheetahs, and thousands of surprisingly swift wildebeests in the signature V-shaped formation. Yes, they do look like they were designed by a committee! It did not take long to better understand rules of nature such as "survival of the fittest." It truly is an unedited reality show. Perhaps growing up on a farm softened the impression of some of the events we witnessed?

After the Serengeti, we journeyed on to the Ngorongoro Crater, with a stop at Olduvai Gorge to study the site of Louis and Mary Leakey's renowned discoveries on the history of early man. After a night at a lodge on the crater's edge, we descended into the crater to view more unique species of wildlife. The seasonal lakes were crowded with brightly colored flamingos as well as many other animals seeking water. We were lucky to see a black rhino, now one of Africa's most endangered animals.

We also witnessed Maasai herdsmen grazing their cattle among the wildlife, just as they have done for centuries. A group of Maasai came to the lodge that evening to share their story with us. My snapshots of the handsome Maasai later served as resource photographs for some of my sculpture pieces.

The following morning we set out via plane to the Samburu National Reserve, stopping over for lunch in Nairobi. The lunch in Nairobi was at the famous Carnivore Restaurant where we dined on various exotic species. It was made clear to us that the animals we were eating had been "ranch raised" and that the profits were applied to help preserve wildlife conditions in the wilds.

At the Samburu National Reserve in Kenya we stayed in surprisingly luxurious tents. We were warned to secure the tents so that no wild varmints might enter. Apparently, the local monkeys had done better in Scouts than we had, as they were more skillful at untying knots than we were at tying them.

Africa / Airbrush / 12" x 16"

Our first trip to Africa, a tour of Kenya and Tanzania, was magical: we viewed an amazing array of wildlife and stayed in stunning surroundings, including the Mount Kenya Safari Club, located on the Equator, facing page. Facing page, inset: Before I even knew I would have the chance to visit the continent, I created this airbrush in an art class in Houston.

The game drives we attended let us see wildlife in such abundance—with such a picturesque intermingling of species—that Everett and I felt as though we were characters in a classic adventure.

We were able to take a hot air balloon ride over the Maasai Mara reserve, left, landing near the Mara River for a champagne brunch. Armed guards protected us from the nearby hippos. Facing page: The panoramic mode of my camera allowed me to capture the stunning vistas we encountered. Below: A milk jug purchased from one of the Samburu huts we visited.

We returned from breakfast to find that they had trashed the place, including unzipping our suitcases and dumping the contents on the floor. I might have been more inclined to forgive if they had been housebroken!

The episode was soon forgotten when we saw reticulated giraffes, Grey's Zebra, and hundreds of bird species throughout the reserve. At the Ewasco Nyiro River we saw crocodiles basking on sunny river banks and elephants mud-bathing. We were able to visit a Samburu village and see their living conditions. We were invited into a very humble hut, where the first thing you saw/smelled was the twenty-four-hour dung fire used for heat and cooking. That said, they were very stately and dignified people.

Before we moved on to Maasai Mara National Reserve (also in Kenya) we stopped for a night at the Mount Kenya Safari Club. The resort is located right on the Equator and offers a great view of Mount Kilimanjaro. We could almost imagine William Holden, Ernest Hemingway, and Ava Gardner sitting at the hotel bar as the Club was a noted retreat for the rich and famous in the 1960s.

Next to the resort was an animal orphanage where I was able to feed ostrich and watch turtles trying to get their share of the food too. The turtles were of such a size that the staff urged me to climb on board for a slug-paced ride, which was great fun.

The Maasai Mara contains large concentrations of big game. It is an ecosystem that has captured the world's attention as a stronghold for African wildlife. There we rode on game drives where we saw accumulations of elephants, giraffes, lions, cheetahs, warthogs, and hyenas. It was great fun seeing the warthogs, with their tails in the air like auto antennae, running along the river's edge among groups of huge elephants. Thrillingly, we experienced a rare sighting: a baby hyena peeking out from a hole in the ground. At first glance the hyenas appear "dog like" but on closer examination you can clearly understand why they are regarded as one of the most vicious and feared animals in Africa. The Maasai Mara also contains numerous large prides of lions. They seemed indifferent to us (in our secure open-air vehicles) and allowed me to get some great lion photos, which I was later able to utilize in some of my oil paintings.

On our last day in Kenya we were up before dawn and off to a hot air balloon flight. Looking down on the animals from high above caused my heart to beat speedily as we viewed the wondrous wildlife arrayed beneath us. I felt no fear throughout the whole balloon flight—until we landed and saw we were near a river full of hippos swimming about. Several opened their huge months and it was then that I realized that if we'd made a different landing, things might have ended badly.

And so ended what was—and remains—my most memorable trip.

In the Samburu village we visited, we were able to enter a family's hut, below, and take portraits of Samburu women, above, and men, right, that later served as reference pieces. Below right: The guides from Abercrombie & Kent provided friendly and knowledgeable attention during our game drives.

Young Samburu Woman / Bronze / 18" tall

Young Samburu Man / Bronze / 18" tall

I still pinch myself when I see the photographs I was able to capture during the game drives. To be able to paint scenes like these that I witnessed with my own eyes is truly a privilege.

King and Queen of the Beasts / Oil on Canvas / 16" x 20"

Time to Rest / Oil on Canvas / 20" x 16"

Cats

Growing up on a farm gave me an appreciation of and love for animals. And I particularly remember adoring our farm cats. Certain members of the family, though, held dissimilar attitudes—especially on the subject of whether they were to be house pets. I recall bringing cats inside and my mother deftly conducting me all the way through to the back door. "They were meant to be in the barn killing mice," was her oft-repeated mantra.

I knew even as a little girl that if I ever had a house of my own I'd have a cat. After my twin sister and I bought a place in Saint Paul's Highland Park, it didn't take long for a little black cat to arrive on the scene—a very muscular cross between a Burmese and a Siamese named Simon. His muscles were put to good use when he wasn't in the mood to be held. If he wasn't, he wasn't. We caught on.

Soon, because friends were moving to Europe and couldn't take their cat, we were "made heir to" a female Siamese named Kitzel. We hadn't consulted Simon first, but they managed to get along. Sweet Kitzel also had a killer instinct. Once, while we watched TV, she flew across the living room chasing a mouse. Another time, even while she was outside on her leash, Kitzel managed to kill a chipmunk.

When Everett and I married we took in Simon and Kitzel. This meant they underwent not only that move, but also many others with us: to a townhouse in Woodbury, then to house on Idsen in Cottage Grove, then to a place on Fawn Trail in Woodbury. We were there at Fawn Trail for only a few months when Simon got very ill. It was so very hard parting with him, my first kitty love.

We had lived in our home on Fawn Trail for only about nine months when we were transferred to Seattle. Another move for Kitzel. She weathered the plane ride fine—that is, with the help of kitty valium. Worked like a charm. It was when we were living on Rhodes End on Bainbridge Island that we decided to get a partner for Kitzel. We wanted another Burmese cat as we had come to think they are the easiest and most loving sort to have with you everyday.

So we found an adorable male Burmese that we named Yoko. And he turned out to be a sweetie of cat; it didn't take long to fall in love with him. But unfortunately he was only with us a very short time when he also became very, very ill. Parting with him was difficult, as it usually is when a pet passes on. Pet owners know—it's almost like having a child.

Kitzel was left alone again, but somehow the Fates intervened. A neighbor at the time knew we'd lost Yoko. She called one day and told me she would be right over. She had something for me. I met her at the car and heard meowing coming from something wrapped inside a blanket. Yes, of course: a kitten. So there was nothing to do but take it inside the house and introduced it to Everett. The new cat was a male tabby, and Everett thought the name Oscar fit him well. I agreed. Oscar proved to be a great cat indeed.

Cats have been my ever-present companions through much of my adult life. My first two cats, Simon and Kitzel, above, came to me before Everett and I were married. In 1994, I commissioned a portrait of Oscar and me as a gift for Everett, facing page.

Oscar and Berry / Oil on Canvas / 18" x 12"

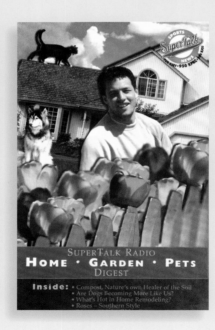

Oscar and Berry hailed from the Pacific Northwest, but they gained their only measure of fame in Houston. I took a photo of Oscar (the tabby) and Berry (the black Burmese) that not only served as reference for a painting but featured prominently in an ad for their vet.

Our cats have been strong supporters of Everett's work, whether it's Oscar curling up in Everett's briefcase while Kitzel camped out on his paperwork, above left, or Berry plopping down on Everett's lap while Oscar napped, above.

As it turns out, however, Oscar and Kitzel didn't have much time together, because Kitzel was starting to get frail. She was a beautiful and loving Siamese that adored sitting on me and taking her paws and kneading me, purring loudly all the while. Often was the time, too, she'd simply plop herself down next to wherever I might be seated and roll her eyes like she was in a sort of ecstatic trance. Kitzel went to kitty heaven in 1983.

As time passed, we decided (as we'd done for other cats in the past) that Oscar needed to have a playmate. We went to Graham, Washington, one day to see if we could find a Burmese that Oscar could be buddies with. We got to the advertised location and saw they had several young kittens. But one cat was a year and a half old—one that the children of the house had, understandably, grown to love and didn't want to sell.

However, this year-and-a-half-old cat jumped right up on my chest in such a way that I automatically had to catch him; he put his paws around my neck and proceeded to rub my ear and purr. Well, that was that! The children surely knew they couldn't keep him forever. After all, weren't they looking for the right people for him? They also could very well see that the animal had chosen me. He was called Royal Raspberry—this, by the way, was his purebred registration name, for he was a show cat who'd won in competition, we were informed, the ribbon for "Best Nurtured." They packed

up some of "Berry's" ribbons to take home with him. We were proud new "show cat" owners.

Oscar and Berry got along very well. It was heartwarming to see them snuggle together. Both had unique and unforgettable qualities. Oscar loved settling in Everett's briefcase when he had left it open on his desk. Many times when we'd go into the bathroom, we'd find Oscar curled up in the sink.

After having lived on Rhodes End for eight years, we decided to have a house built on Agate Beach Lane, on the north end of Bainbridge Island. We'd sold the Rhodes End residence, and—because construction "ran long" on the new house—we had to find a place to live in the meantime. A house opened up for us on Beans Bight at the south end of the island.

The Beans Bight place was an older home that came furnished. And (as we later found out) there were a lot of nooks, cracks, and crannies where Oscar and Berry could explore—or sometimes even disappear. Beyond those

Oscar, above, and Berry, left,
traveled with us from Bainbridge
Island to Houston—remaining
lovable regardless of residence.

adventures, we at times wondered why both kitties seemed so entirely intrigued by a few of the already-hung pictures on the wall. We sometimes found them tapping or patting at the corners of them with their paws. In time we discovered bats behind those pictures.

But we finally moved away from that place and all its built-in delights for the cats and settled into our new home on Agate Beach Lane. I have a fond memory of winters there, when we'd have the woodburning stove going and the cats would get as close as they could to it.

We had lived there for only about two and a half years when Everett came home one evening and announced that work had offered up the opportunity to move to Houston. Well, Oscar and Berry were Washington State natives. But by the way they'd cozied up to our stove in winter, we convinced ourselves they'd take to the Texan sun like moths to a flame.

For the trip south Oscar and Berry stowed away in "coat storage" on the company plane.

As we hoped they would, Oscar and Berry loved their new home and the warm, sunny weather. While in Texas, we found ourselves traveling quite a bit. We hunted for the best place to board the two "darlings" during these times. It was the Memorial Cat Hospital, where Dr. Folger was the owner and vet. He was a wonderful guy who came to love our cats, as did all his assistants. I had of course taken many pictures of "my dears," Oscar and Berry. One time, I framed one of my favorites and offered it to Dr. Folger. He liked it so much he asked—to my utter delight—if he could use it in his advertisements.

Oscar was one of the biggest cats we'd had. Big, meaning plump. It was a continual struggle keeping his weight under control. It meant feeding each cat different foods and keeping them out of the other dish. Everett teased Oscar, calling him Bubba. Which of course was rude, but the cat suffered the insult well, still devotedly remaining by Everett's side every chance he got.

Berry was an amazingly loving cat. Just as when we two got formally introduced, believe it or not, there wasn't a day that went by when he didn't jump up on me, put his paws around my neck, then rub my right ear and purr. In fact, some days he would go through this routine more than was strictly necessary. But that didn't matter to him—and once he made up his mind, there was no getting around it. Hence, we dubbed him with the nickname "Love Love."

Not all cat owners do this, but I'd bathe the cats. Berry got so used to it, he'd even (in fact, almost always) fall to sleep during this routine. Oscar liked the drying off part better (I used a hair dryer).

When Oscar was fourteen, we got the sad news from Dr. Folger that our beloved cat was very ill and there was nothing that could be done for him. It was a gloomy day for all of us, even Dr. Folger. I could see it on his face. After Oscar passed on, since the two cats had been as peas in a pod, Berry had some adjustments to make too. I recall him clinging to me for a long while. So sad. Then, in time, he finally got used to the idea of being our one and only family pet. King of the roost wasn't all that horrible a position to be in.

Everett retired in 1999. We stayed in Houston for a year after that but then decided to head back north to Bainbridge Island. Berry was to face (and perfectly well endure) yet another plane ride. In time, as is the way of life, even Berry was starting to show his age. We did everything we could think of to make him comfortable. Everett thought that maybe he would like lying on a heating pad, and that was the perfect solution. The cat loved it. Berry lived over twenty-one years, a long time for any cat. He was the most adorable and lovable friend— qualities that made it terribly rough parting with him. He'll always have an exceptionally bright place in our hearts.

Two years passed without pets. One day, Everett said, "Bernie, I see they have an eight-year-old Siamese named

Angel at PAWS. Let's go see what we think." Angel was at a foster home at the time, but they had other cats there too. There were two tiny black-cat brothers (one with white whiskers) snuggled together in a cage that was positioned near the front door. Everett asked if I wanted to hold one of those two caged kitties. And, well, that's all it took; we quickly had two new little kitties. Both, by the way, were born on the Fourth of July, so we later had occasion to refer to them as the "little fire crackers."

But first we had to give them official names. One of them was meant to be Max, because Everett and I both said "Max" at the same time. As for what to call the second little dear, Everett and I promised each other we'd sleep on. However, before I went to bed for some reason I scribbled down the name Matt on a sheet of paper. The next morning, amazingly, Everett said, "I think Matt would be a good name." These kitties were destined to be Matt and Max.

In no time at all (and it never seems to take too long), Matt and Max were big fellers. Even though they were brothers, how different their personalities were: Max was more loving to people while Matt remained aloof and skittered out of sight whenever anyone came over. When Everett and I would both be about to leave the house for a bit, we got into the habit of putting Matt and Max in the bedroom and closing the door. (There was plenty of room in there after all, and windows for them to look out.) In time, all we'd need to say was "lockdown," and both of them knew what we meant. Matt would consistently run into the room. Max—well, he'd cooperate depending upon his mood that day.

These two brothers were able to translate into some sort of "catspeak" other things Everett said. For instance, when upstairs watching television, he'd call out, "Where are my tubing buddies?" At that, Matt and Max would scamper upstairs and make themselves comfortable in their usual positions on the ottoman next to his chair.

Although these kitty brothers were discernibly different in personality, they tragically shared the same genetic defect, which we learned about in the last year they

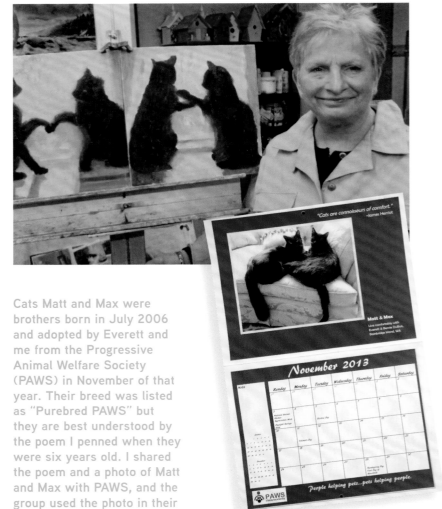

The Bainbridge Boys

Two cats named Matt and Max were adopted from PAWS for
The major cause to bring love to their owners

Matt is a little fat and Max is the opposite of that
Matt has a tail that is always up in the air while Max
Has one that looks like it is fluffy and full of air

They are brothers but Max has long hair and Matt
Has short as the breed is really hard to sort
They are black but while in the sun they turn brown

Sometimes the chase is on as they run for the fun
And other times to settle a dispute
However, as cats they still think that rest is best

They are smart as one rolls over on command
and the other in demand
We always give them permission to accomplish their mission
As love is a precious gift we give each other

Cats Matt and Max were brothers born in July 2006 and adopted by Everett and me from the Progressive Animal Welfare Society (PAWS) in November of that year. Their breed was listed as "Purebred PAWS" but they are best understood by the poem I penned when they were six years old. I shared the poem and a photo of Matt and Max with PAWS, and the group used the photo in their 2013 calendar.

were with us—a most heartrending time. The both of them left us in August 2013. They'll forever have, though, a cherished place in our hearts.

By the way, Matt and Max starred in the PAWS "Pet-of-the-Month" calendar for November 2013. I'd sent in a photograph I'd taken of them, along with a poem I'd written about them. Don't they make a fine pair!

As Everett and I started to plan our fortieth wedding anniversary in 2016, we decided that we didn't want to travel anywhere but did want to mark this milestone with a special gift. That gift came in the form of Winter and Fiona. We joked that we'd acquired a boyfriend for me and a girlfriend for Everett. They are Ragdolls in the true sense of the word.

Winter, above left, and Fiona, above, came from a breeder in Seattle in 2016. They are Ragdolls, a breed known for their extreme interest in people. From their desire to follow me from room to room, these two are true to character.

Reaching the Summit

3

Marilyn / Clay / 9" tall

Our Northwest Return

In 1999, when Everett decided to retire, we considered moving to a number of places around the country but ultimately settled on returning to Bainbridge Island. We bought a house on Lafayette Avenue, on the north end of the island near Fay Bainbridge Park. In 2005 we added a condo in downtown Seattle as a city getaway.

I turned the bottom floor of our Lafayette home into my studio. It was a wonderful space, with windows that faced out to the water. When Ed Hankey came to visit, he helped me set up a small kiln and I worked on a few pieces there. I soon realized, though, that I preferred to work in a facility where I could not only dip my pieces in glaze but also work alongside others. I missed having someone to critique my work, fellow artists to work with, and a group to be around.

To me the most fun—the best thing—is a challenge. And learning new things is challenging. I don't want to get stagnant. I like to have my own style and own ideas, and sometimes I do things a little bit differently, but art classes have always been the best way for me to keep fresh and current and inspired.

Bainbridge's parks department operated a pottery studio in Eagledale Park, so I decided to sign up for some classes. The sculpture classes were taught by Shirley Burns, who taught in the way I find most conducive to learning: I really like to watch an instructor demonstrate a new technique, and then I like to be given time to work on my own until I run into a problem. If I have an issue or there seems to be something that I'm totally lost on, I will ask the instructor for help. I really appreciate it when they are willing to demonstrate again for me so that I can do the hands-on work myself. With Shirley I did a number of pieces of faces that I continue to be proud of.

In my Lafayette studio I focused on my painting. A woman in nearby Poulsbo, Julann Campbell, operated

When we decided to return to Bainbridge Island following Everett's retirement, I missed my friends from Houston terribly. Again, art was my salvation. One of the first sculptures I created was a figure depicting Marilyn Woodruff, facing page far left, which helped me process my feelings of loss. I also forged new friendships in Shirley Burns and Julann Campbell's classes. Facing page near left: A trip to the lavender fields in Sequim with Julann (second from left) and fellow students. Left: A piece I produced on the Sequim trip.

Lavender Field in Sequim / Oil on Canvas / 10" x 14"

classes out of her home studio. I appreciated the perspective Julann offered on my work, and I liked the camaraderie of her classes. Julann is, in my opinion, probably one of the best artists on the planet, and her classes provided a lot of opportunity for what I think is the only way I can truly learn: through feedback.

I love critiquing. I like having someone tell me what's wrong with what I'm doing. For me that's the best way. I'm not there to just throw something together and think it's good right away. I love feedback that helps make my artwork better—in fact, I've always loved feedback in everything in my life. And I really appreciated the caliber of artists who met at Julann's studio. I liked being in their energy, being around their art. There weren't that many artists around that were as good as they were and really consistent. They would critique my work if I asked for a critique, and they were honest with me.

The years I painted with Julann were a very focused time in my life. I would go there every week. It was a set time, and I never let anything else interfere.

I loved the drive down Big Valley Road to get to Julann's. I also loved knowing that I had a set time to do this because it signaled to Everett—and to me—that this was a day that was really important. When Everett was working I knew that supporting him by making meals, keeping the house up, and entertaining had to come first. Any art classes I took were usually for an hour or two in the middle of the day, when I was sure it wouldn't interfere with my responsibilities. Now that Everett was retired, I was leaving at about 9:30 and not getting back until 5 o'clock. As such, our return to Bainbridge ushered in the most prolific period of my career.

Autumn in Minnesota / Oil on Canvas / 24" x 18"

Mystical Clouds / Oil on Canvas / 18" x 14"

While figures were a primary focus of my paintings and sculpture during the years we lived in Houston, landscapes, cityscapes, interiors, and still life came to dominate my painting after our return to Bainbridge. The Pacific Northwest provided an abundance of inspiring scenery, as did visits back to the Midwest.

Clouds at Sunrise / Oil on Canvas / 12" x 9"

Hidden Beauty / Oil on Canvas / 12" x 9"

Washington Scenery / Oil on Canvas / 12" x 9"

Taking sculpting classes with Shirley Burns offered me the chance to make new connections on the island and develop my skills in new and exciting directions. Left: Shirley's sculpting class, circa 2000, included (front row, from left) Nancy Fraychineaud, me, Madge Confrey, Georgia Angus, (back row, from left) Marilyn Dooley, Shirley Burns, Fran Phillips, and Jason Parker.

Reflections on Bernie

by Shirley Burns

I worked at the Parks department for a number of years. I had been an art teacher in Virginia and Pennsylvania and then taught at North Kitsap High School before coming to work with the Parks department in 1984. I first taught the children's classes, then adult classes, and then I shifted to sculpture. Bernie was one of my sculpture students.

I realized Bernie had previous experience and had accomplished quite a lot before joining my class. I usually presented a technique and students were free to respond in whatever way they chose. However, I always announced that if people had their own ideas of what they wanted to do, they should feel free to do so. More often than not, that is the way Bernie worked. She likes working on faces—shoulders, neck, and head—and brought in sketches to follow, completing a piece every two weeks or so.

Bernie was self-motivated, and she seemed happy and relaxed in doing her work. I think she enjoyed focusing on a project she had in mind. She had very good ideas, had a high standard for herself and was very conscious of what she wanted to achieve, and did in fact accomplish what she

hoped. She was very professional in her approach to her own work.

Bernie was most enthusiastic and delighted the group with her enthusiasm. She brought skills to the ten-member group, and I think she was an inspiration to people who were getting started. And she was very supportive of other people's efforts: she encouraged people and was a very positive asset to the class, which developed a sort of camaraderie over time. Bernie always seemed pleased about discussion about her work. She welcomed feedback, accepted it very cheerfully, and made adjustments when she wanted to.

Although Bernie is known in the community more for her paintings than her sculpture, I know she enjoys her pieces. She told me that she has used them throughout her home and very much enjoys looking at them and remembering the classes and what she accomplished there.

Bernie and I remain friends to this day, visiting together over lunch. Bernie is a wonderfully enthusiastic person, delightful to bump into. She sort of radiates the sunshine.

Bernie's Artifact / Clay / 12" tall

Tibetan Girl / Clay / 9" tall

Grandma / Clay / 10" tall

Maple Leaf / Clay / 7" wide

Wind Fall / Clay / 6" wide

Elsa / Clay / 10" tall

Friends / Clay / 9" tall

In Shirley's class, I challenged myself to develop a different approach to sculpture—I wanted to create more art purely from my imagination. The pieces at top left, above, and left were all produced purely from my mind's eye rather than any reference material.

Northwest Indian

The inspiration for sculpting the Northwest Indian head came when we were living at our Port Madison waterfront home on Bainbridge Island. I was intrigued by the Suquamish people I could see clamming along the tide flats. As I watched them working I realized that I had lived in the Northwest for several years and had not yet used the native people as subject matter. That created a sudden urgency within me—I really needed to do it.

Producing the sculpture was both challenging and enjoyable. It was particularly difficult to find references that would work for me. I visited the Suquamish Tribal Center as well as the local library in search of paintings and photos, but I had trouble finding imagery that depicted Native American faces from the various angles I needed. When I found the feathers to use for the design, though, the creative process took over and I was able to complete the piece in my downstairs studio in under a week.

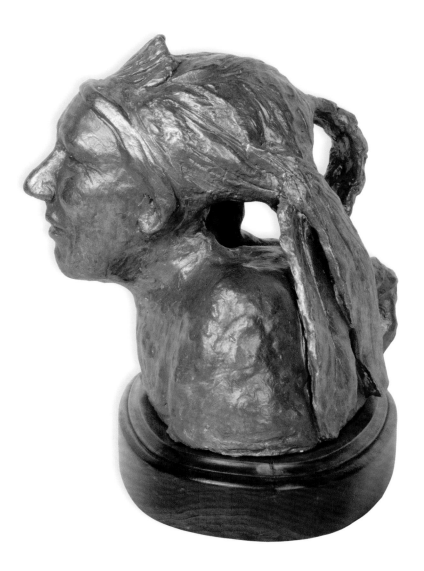

After a long search for reference material that could provide all the angles I needed, the sculpting of my Northwest Indian piece went quickly. I was particularly pleased with how the feathers came out.

Northwest Indian / Clay / 13" tall

My Space to Create

After leaving Houston to return to Bainbridge Island, I wanted a workspace where I could continue my oil painting and sculpture. The house we bought on Lafayette Avenue, on the far north end of the island, had the perfect solution: a daylight basement that I immediately knew would be the perfect studio—and it was.

My studio had a path that came down and around from the front of the house to its own entrance, and the studio itself had a wonderful view of our rolling lawn, a dock where birds and otters would play, and the Point Monroe sandspit. We put in track lighting and shelving and had a workbench built, and I placed my monoprint press and some of my sculptures there. While visiting from Houston, Ed Hankey helped me install a small kiln in the garage.

The Lafayette studio was a wonderful spot to paint and find inspiration—it was while looking out my studio window that I had the idea for my Northwest Indian sculpture. It also had enough room for me to welcome others to work alongside me—either in the studio or out on the lawn. Julann Campbell used my studio to teach a class on watercolor to a handful of students, including me.

Everett and I loved our home on Lafayette, but eventually the large home, dock, and yard became too much to keep up with. After I wound up on crutches due to a stress fracture and saw Everett out there doing the weeding, I knew we needed to make a change. In 2008, we decided to find a condo for us and a new studio for me.

I found what I thought would be a great space on Madison Avenue, walking distance from our new condo on Parfitt Way. The commercial building was shared by Billy Shears, where I had my hair cut, and a small gift shop run by a nice lady. We painted the concrete floor a tropical eggshell blue, which I've come to call "Bernie's Blue"; created a nice sitting area with a rug, comfortable chairs, and a coffee table; and installed the workbench and matching stools as well as a nice desk of Everett's that he had in Houston.

Although the studio was close by and I enjoyed interacting with the other tenants, the space was not ideal. Because of all that I needed to carry back and forth between my home and studio, I often ended up driving the short distance—only to find the parking spaces in front of my entrance full. The biggest disappointment with this space, however, was when it flooded with rainwater almost two years after I moved in. In addition to soaking a beautiful big area rug, the water destroyed a number of books—as well as several plaster molds I'd saved from my sculptures. It was devastating. When our lease was expiring, Everett had someone start looking for a new space.

What was found was an office on Ericksen Avenue that was bright, located on the ground floor, and with ample parking. I absolutely loved the bright, bustling space. I was able to pick out the paint—one wall was painted Bernie's Blue, of course—and almost all of the furniture that had been in the studio on Madison fit perfectly. I had a person build large shelves on rollers (also painted Bernie's Blue), and there I stored all of my framed works. The sitting area served not only as a pleasant place for me to pause from my work—which in this studio has been mostly organizing my work for various shows and for my book project—but also for Everett to host friends for coffee or one of his board meetings.

When I look back at the three studios I've had over the past fifteen years, I feel lucky to have worked in such bright yet soothing spaces and proud of the energy I've put into creating them.

I had two other workspaces before moving to my studio on Ericksen Avenue, facing page. Our home on Lafayette, top left, had a daylight basement that I transformed into a studio space. Fellow artists, top right and right, would sometimes paint with me in our backyard, which looked out on Port Madison. Above: After we moved to our condo, I rented this studio space on Madison Avenue.

In addition to wonderful friends and inspiring locales, Bainbridge Island has provided me with a series of bright, stimulating workspaces. Here, my studio on Ericksen Avenue is shown.

Beholding Empires

In July of 2001, Everett and I embarked on a tour to Budapest, Prague, and Vienna and then followed that up with a ten-day Scandinavian cruise loop departing from Copenhagen. The trip offered us a chance to discover the history, layout, and architecture of each spot we saw and get a feel for the sensibilities of its residents. Last but (of course) not least were the many sumptuous collections of proudly displayed art we got to see at many of these major stopovers. I won't soon forget them.

Budapest is stunningly beautiful. I retain in my mind's eye the many wondrous spires and church façades that cry out to be painted there. However at the time of our travels to this Hungarian capital (its largest city), it was in the midst of blending its previous Communist rule with newer capitalist ideas. The result (which I could see in its old versus new architectural styles) could be described as a sort of nonviolent chaos.

We next came to Vienna; that city easily won my heart, for it's a place steeped in music, art, and so many other forms of culture. We had a tour of the Schloss Schönbrunn Palace, the Habsburg Dynasty's summer residence. We visited the city's fantastically impressive opera house and attended an evening of classical music—although, at a nearby site. Vienna was the proud home of Gustav Klimt's golden paintings—rich and splendid as they are!

Then we were off to do a brief cruise on the Danube. And after that, to Prague. We made a stop at the Melk Abbey, where our necks ached from craning up at hundreds of gold-topped pilasters and ceilings quite busy with paintings. Melk is billed as one of the greatest abbeys in Europe (and you'd get no argument from me). Because Prague had avoided the destruction of the two world wars, we were able to wander through unscathed town squares, see spire-studded skylines, and even drink in medieval architecture. Sipping coffee at a sidewalk café, I easily pictured myself in Prague during its nineteenth-century artistic heyday.

After Prague, we were slated for Copenhagen in order to begin our Princess line cruise. After a day and night at sea we arrived in Stockholm. We saw Stockholm's Vasa Museum, walked Old Town, and toured the City Hall known for its well-appointed Blue Hall where Nobel Prizes are handed out. We next embarked for Helsinki and saw its colorful Market Square and the almost otherworldly Temppeliaukio Church, which was carved out of solid rock and topped with a huge interior copper dome.

Our next stop was Saint Petersburg. To me, this was the highlight of our trip. To take in its massive body of art and glorious edifices is equivalent to drinking from a fire hose. We spent time at the Catherine Palace, viewed the Church of the Savior on the Spilled Blood, and walked down many picturesque streets. At first blush Saint Petersburg presents as being mightily impressive indeed. This was Vladimir Putin's birthplace, so it has been rewarded with substantial funds for infrastructure improvements. We also came to notice that, when you look behind the initial façade, life for many of its residents appeared to be difficult.

We took in Saint Petersburg's Palace Square in front of the Hermitage—built in the eighteenth century during the reign of Catherine the Great. The Winter Palace and four adjacent buildings contain more than one thousand rooms and halls. Although security and the facility conditions weren't at a level you'd see in some other of the world's more famous museums, this place is to Saint Petersburg what the Louvre is to Paris. What art it holds! The spectacular collections included pieces by painters whose names, you won't be surprised, sounded vaguely familiar to me: Da Vinci, Raphael, Michelangelo, Rembrandt, El Greco, Goya, Van Gogh, Matisse, Rubens, Renoir, and Monet.

That evening we experienced one of my favorite passions, the ballet. It was an impressive production of *Swan Lake*, put on at the Alexandrinsky Theatre. From Saint Petersburg we hopped back on our cruise ship and sailed to

Our second trip to Europe gave us the chance to delve into the Austro-Hungarian and Scandinavian cultures. Clockwise from top left: our wonderful cruise staff; the Alexander Nevsky Cathedral in Tallinn; the Schönbrunn Palace outside Vienna; a photo Everett took of me on the Charles Bridge in Prague; and Everett and me in a Benedictine monastery garden.

the city of Tallinn in Estonia, where we explored (among other things) the fantastical Alexander Nevsky Cathedral, Tallinn's largest orthodox cupola cathedral.

We then sailed to Gdynia, the gateway port for the city of Gdańsk, Poland. It was here that on September 1, 1939, the first shots were fired that marked the beginning of WWII. Later, in 1970, food riots at the Lenin Shipyard gave birth to Poland's Solidarity movement.

We toured Gdańsk, followed by a trip through colorful country landscape to the Malbork Castle, one of Poland's largest, most popular, and oldest (construction began in 1274) Gothic complexes. We learned that the castle was acquired by the government in the 1800s and has undergone extensive restoration since; so it's done well for itself after the ravages

of WWII. The guided tour of Malbork Castle, with its many rich collections, included the marvel of countless interior columns that, at their top ends, splayed up and out like giant lilies to connect with the towering ceilings above.

Next was Oslo, the oldest of the Scandinavian capitals—a city that covers a large land area, giving its inhabitants plenty of space. It was a blend of nineteenth- and twentieth-century architectural styles. We visited the Vigelandsparken, a sculpture park filled with more than two hundred pieces of Gustav Vigeland's work. Of course, it was a must-see. Now there's a man after my own heart! He created a wonder world of human figures and animals in stone, iron, and bronze, each a striking depiction of a facet of the entire range of human life—from birth to man's struggles and trials, then to death. This park was great inspiration for me.

Our trip was, sadly, over when we finally disembarked from our ship in Copenhagen. The feel of the art we saw on this trip nearly overpowers me when I think back on it. There was variety beyond expectations, ranging from the dark yet serene orthodox grandness of the Alexander Nevsky Cathedral to the modern symbolism of the mammoth figures either at play or in some form of angst at Oslo's Vigeland Sculpture Park. When I think that I witnessed the remarkably competent elegance of the Russian ballet as well as the sheer volume of old masters at the Hermitage, I guess my "takeaway" is simple enough: Art exhilarates!

OIL PAINTINGS

Oil painting is near and dear to my heart. It is something I have done for years, and every time I pick up the paintbrush and start painting I find I am lost in time. It has been great therapy over the years, as it helps me to forget my physical condition.

Over the years I've been blessed with many great teachers who have taught me what I have needed to be the artist I am today. In my heart, I have a high level of gratitude for all the knowledge they have shared and their honesty in critiquing my work. For me, this was a very important part of my learning process.

I love the fluid expressive technique that I get with oil paints, I found it to be a very forgiving medium where I could draw the subject matter on the canvas with my paintbrush, and make corrections as needed. It didn't matter what style of painting I was trying to achieve—it was always possible with oil paints.

It is amazing how many oil paints there are to choose from today. When I first started oil painting, the only way I could achieve some of the colors was by learning how to mix colors. It is still my favorite way to do it, but that doesn't mean that I don't have just about every color you can think of having in your toolbox. Every now and then I would treat myself, but I have to be careful not to overindulge.

The more I learned about oil painting the more it carried through in my appreciation for art. It has certainly been a blessing when I had the many opportunities to tour art museums all over the world. One of my many favorites was going to Monet's home in Giverny. I guess it's my love of flowers, nature, and of the impressionistic style of painting that made it so special.

Oil paints are my favorite two-dimensional medium.
They are slow to dry, allowing me to take my time.
I painted this scene of a cello at the Olympic Music
Festival in the late 2000s.

Cello at Olympic Music Festival / Oil on Canvas / 16" x 20"

The ferry ride between our homes on Bainbridge Island and downtown Seattle provides not only a serene commute but sometimes the opportunity to spot marine life. I personally have been blessed with many great sightings of orcas migrating through Puget Sound. Here, I depict a pod of orcas passing through Elliott Bay, the inspiration for which came from a local newspaper photo.

Migration / Oil on Canvas / 30" x 15"

Images that touch my soul, like the image of the two boys in Tibet, as well as life around me have provided some of the greatest inspirations for my oil paintings.

Anybody Home / Oil on Canvas / 11" x 14"

Children in Tibet / Oil on Canvas / 20" x 16"

Girl at Olympic Music Festival / Oil on Canvas / 12" x 16"

Manor Farm / Oil on Canvas / 20" x 16"

Battle Point #1 / Oil on Canvas / 12" x 12"

Battle Point #2 / Oil on Canvas / 12" x 12"

Battle Point #3 / Oil on Canvas / 12" x 12"

The Pioneer Square Pergola in Winter / Oil on Canvas / 24" x 20"

Bay Hay and Feed Gazebo / Oil on Canvas / 20" x 16"

Front Street Bar / Oil on Canvas / 20" x 16"

Local establishments have also been a source of inspiration for my oil paintings. Left: The warmth and activity of Rolling Bay Café. Above: Front Street Bar in Port Townsend.

Rolling Bay Cafe / Oil on Canvas / 24" x 18"

The activity of Seattle's waterfront has provided endless scenes to capture in oil.

Trip to Seattle / Oil on Canvas / 16" x 20"

View From Pike Place Market / Oil on Canvas / 16" x 20"

Reflections on Bernie

by Julann Campbell

Bernie DuBois is really an interesting student, and she's become a very kind and attentive friend. When Bernie began taking oil painting classes from me in my home studio in the early 2000s, it was clear to me that Bernie wanted to learn and grow and get better. She was really willing to hear what needed work or what was strong and then go from there. And in so doing, she's just gotten really so much better.

Bernie is able to look at something, replicate it, and do it not only well, but quickly. Her color is really quite good also. Bernie can design her own projects and has, in all different mediums. Whenever she's wanted to do a piece in a different medium, she's seen to it that she learns how to do it. Whether it's a painting, whether it's her ceramics or sculpture, whether it's collage or encaustics, in everything Bernie does she goes all out and does it 100 percent.

There's been a group of us that has painted for many, many years together. My class was held once a week all year long, and it was just a very regular group, with Michael Graham and John Campbell. With Bernie it was always hugs and kisses all the way around—when she got there and when she left. However, it was not uncommon for her to say, "Now, don't work too much further, because you could mess it up. It looks really good now, Mike." She absolutely always provided her fellow students a good critique. And she really wanted a critique of her own work: it wasn't that she was here just for fun and games.

We did have a good time, of course. We would all bring a sack lunch and take a break for lunch. When the weather was nice, we'd go out and do plein air work, and Bernie was always game for that. Most recently we were up at the lavender fields in Sequim. We rented a house for a week and went out painting every day. And then, when we were burnt out and tired at the end of the day, we'd go out for dinner and have a glass of wine. She also painted with that group in Port Gamble. There, she sold the painting she was working on. This lady had marched across the street to our group, asked if she could look at the paintings, and fell in love with the painting Bernie did of her house. She bought it on the spot.

Bernie has always had a mind for business as well as art. She has hung her work in different galleries on the island for years and has done well at the golf club she and Everett belong to. We'd hung as a group way back when they were much younger, and one of my excitements was to see my students become professionals.

Bernie is someone who is just driven to use her time wisely. She has many interests, and whatever she does, she does it beautifully. She designed her kitchen, from the pulls on the drawers and the doors to the colors—everything. What one would usually hire an interior designer for, she made those decisions, every single one of them. It's the same way in her former studio. She painted the cement floors the most beautiful tropical green you've ever seen, kind of a turquoise green. The whole place was just so beautifully done.

No matter what it is she's designing, Bernie goes full bore. She's not one to just sit down and do nothing; she has to be busy and use her time well. That's Bernie.

Lavender Field / Oil on Canvas / 10" x 10"

Pistachio in Still Life / Oil on Masonite / 24" x 30"

Pewter and Pansies / Oil on Canvas / 12" x 16"

Still Life

Painting still life has certainly been part of my learning experience. Much can be learned in painting a still life. Sometimes it can be challenging but, as with so many pursuits, worth the patience to learn. Over the years I have found that the special part of painting still life is incorporating objects into my piece that I cherish.

Composition is very important when doing a still life. The way the light hits the objects is the key concern. I found that a critical part of making a still life great is showing how the reflection of one object shows up in another, usually a metal or highly polished item.

Artists have been painting still lifes for centuries. Typically their subject matter is made up entirely of inanimate objects—hence the "still" in still life. That has been the case for all of my pieces in this genre with the exception of one. Each time I focused on capturing a scene composed of flowers, a mirror, a painting of a young girl, and a chair, Julann Campbell's cat, Pistachio, would saunter in and sit down in the chair. It didn't take long for me to realize that she was determined to be part of my painting. Between my love of cats and appreciation for such a willing model, I was thrilled.

The work I did, primarily with Julann Campell, on still lifes is some of my favorite. For many pieces I focused on my favorite objects of beauty, flowers. All the subject matter, usually composed for our class by Julann, fascinated me. Working on still lifes allowed me to focus on light and texture in a way that I had not in my earlier work.

Still Life with Red Umbrella / Oil on Canvas / 24" x 24"

Still Life with Onions / Oil on Canvas / 24" x 24"

Still Life with Poppies / Oil on Canvas / 24" x 24"

Fascination with Pottery / Oil on Canvas / 18" x 18"

Tea Time / Oil on Masonite / 24" x 16"

Still Life of Pears / Oil on Canvas / 16" x 12"

Morning Coffee / Oil on Canvas / 24" x 24"

Pottery Piece from Mother / Oil on Canvas / 36" x 24"

Oranges and Lemons / Oil on Canvas / 16" x 12"

Grandfather's Clock / Oil on Canvas / 36" x 24"

Among the amazing experiences Everett and I had on our trip to China was our visit to Xian, where we looked down on trenches filled with excavated life-sized sculptures of soldiers.

Our Journey to China

Magic happens in the strangest ways. Two friends and I were out enjoying the day on the Kitsap Peninsula when the rain became so heavy that we decided to pull into the Elandan Gardens parking lot. I had never been there before. We went in and, much to my surprise, they had a large collection of Chinese artifacts. They informed me of the tours they do every year to China and that they had one scheduled for April with space available for two more people. Before I knew it a brochure was tucked under my arm, and I was told they would love to have me join them. The deadline for finalizing the trip gave us only two days to decide. Both Everett and I decided it looked like it would be a great trip.

Dan and Diane Robinson, the owners of Elandan Gardens, were escorting us on the trip. They had a special party at their home for all of us who were taking the trip with them. Their knowledge of the best guides combined with so many pleasant people signed up for the tour, assured us of a great trip. We also knew this would be the last chance to see the ancient Yangtze River, before it would be altered by the Three Gorges Dam. In April 2003, we embarked on a trip with people we had met, and whose company we knew we would enjoy.

After arriving at Beijing we started by having a day at the market. We figured it would be crowded, but what we wandered into was far more than we could have ever expected. Seeing that many people in one place was overwhelming, but in time we would get used to seeing that many people.

The next day we had a full-day tour of Tiananmen Square, the Forbidden City, the Temple of Heaven, and the Summer Palace. Unfortunately, they had a windstorm and the air quality was as bad as it got at that time. That evening we had a dinner of, appropriately enough, Peking duck.

We were thrilled that when we went to the Beijing Zoo the pandas were outside. This gave all of us a chance to get great pictures. We couldn't imagine going to a zoo in China and not coming home with a picture of a panda. (For me, this was especially hoped for since there was always the possibility of a future painting or sculpture coming out of a picture I'd taken.)

I would consider one of the highlights of the China trip our visit to the Great Wall. Everett and I walked and climbed further than we expected. The Great Wall is considered one of the greatest man-made sites on earth. On the way back to Beijing we visited the Ming tombs, where more than a dozen emperors have been buried.

We had a full day at Xian, which is the city made famous by the discovery of the buried Terra Cotta Army, more than six thousand life-sized warriors and horses made of clay. This was one of my very favorite days. Even as I looked at this famous site, the extent of it seemed beyond my comprehension. It was my love for sculpture and terra cotta clay that made it so special. We also drove through the countryside to the "terra cotta digs," where many archeological finds have been made, including the displayed soldiers. In addition to all of this, we had the opportunity to meet the farmer who discovered the terra cotta warriors when he was working his farm. He signed a brochure and we got to have our pictures taken with him.

We flew from Xian to Chongqing—a city that became famous during WWII as the western terminal used by the supply planes. Here we had the opportunity to visit the local "Artist Colony." We all had a great time meeting artists skilled in many different mediums. Everett and I were thrilled when we found two fabulous oil paintings done by a local art instructor. One of them was of a young Chinese boy and the other of a young Chinese girl—both in the traditional garments. They took them out of the frames and rolled the canvases up, so they could be put in a tube. Luckily, we got them home safely and took them to a gallery here and had them framed. They are so special that we have them hanging where we can enjoy them every day.

From here we embarked on an exciting cruise down the Yangtze River. One first shore excursion was named "City of Ghosts." After cruising through the night we arrived at Wushan where we transferred to a smaller boat for a voyage entitled "Three Small Gorges."

The Three Gorges Dam, the world's largest hydropower project, was being built in Xiling Gorge on the western border of Hubei Province. At that time the estimated cost, in US currency, was $60 billion. We visited the diversion channel, Xiling Bridge, the model of the dam, and Tangling (the highest place of the dam site) to see the overall view of the construction site. To see this and to imagine how many people were going to be affected by this was incredible.

We then took a most pleasurable fifteen-hour boat trip down the Li River. The famous rock formations that we saw, the Old Man Mountain, Nine Horse Hill, and Crescent Hill, were breathtaking. The Li River has the most picturesque scenery in China—it's one of the top ten watery wonders of the world.

Nearing the end of the trip, we flew to Shanghai with its population (in 2003) of 11 million. By now, it's grown to 24 million. We met a national guide who took us to the Garden of Happiness (Yu Yuan), the Shanghai Museum, and one of the many silk factories. It was very intriguing, as there was the cutest young Chinese boy feeding the caterpillar larvae chopped mulberry leaves.

Throughout the time we were there I was able to snap some adorable pictures of children. I particularly loved the picture I got of two young girls out with their family. I later captured them in one of my oil paintings, What fun!

It was amazing to see and be in the midst of a culture I had previously known so little about. This was meaningful to me since I have so many lovely Chinese friends. The trip offered me a deeper appreciation for them, their heritage, and their many traditions.

After returning from our trip we had a nearly insurmountable number of great photographs that we managed to wrestle into two wonderful albums. An added incentive to quickly completing the albums was the knowledge that the members of the tour group were all getting together after the trip to share our memories. At the gathering we all shared stories with each other, and looked at each other's photo albums. It all made for a great evening as people who were strangers just a month earlier were now friends talking about a common experience. There were many interesting people on the trip, and it resulted in some lasting friendships.

Sisters' Day Out / Oil on Canvas / 12" x 12"

I loved the opportunity to see icons like the Great Wall, below right, or Tiananmen Square and native giant pandas, facing page. However, it was the smaller moments—like spotting an adorable pair of sisters in matching sweaters, below left—that offered material for my art.

Hummingbirds #1 / Oil on Canvas / 16" x 12"

Hummingbirds

Living where there are hummingbirds all year long gives me the joy and privilege of seeing them often. I need only to look out on our deck to see them enjoying the nectar of the flowers I've grown.

Painting hummingbirds gives me great joy because they are one of my favorite birds. I find their ability to move their little wings at such speed inspiring. Plus, people tell me hummingbirds remind them of me: small, in constant motion, and a bit feisty.

Hummingbirds #2 / Oil on Canvas / 12" x 12"

Hummingbirds #3 / Oil on Canvas / 12" x 12"

Hummingbirds #4 / Oil on Canvas / 12" x 12"

Hummingbirds #5 / Oil on Canvas / 12" x 12"

Exploring Peru and the Galápagos

After hearing so many fascinating things that friends had been telling us about Machu Picchu and the Galápagos Islands, we decided to take a peek at some of the brochures. Being able to visit the Charles Darwin Research Station to learn of the efforts to preserve the Galápagos Islands and then to also see Machu Picchu sounded most exciting to us.

Our October 2004 trip started with a trip to Lima, Peru, to view its diverse culture. We saw the Plaza Mayor at the center of the city, encircled by the Government Palace, Cathedral of Lima, Archbishop's Palace, and the Palace of the Union. Seeing soldiers guarding the Government Palace and watching them perform some of their drills was stirring.

After seeing historical Lima, we drove through the modern part of the city, where the residential areas had awesome views of the Pacific Ocean. Then we stopped at the National Museum of Archaeology—back to history—and how that museum fascinated me. I was especially captivated by learning the progression of the Inca culture from as far back as 1200 BC.

The next day we flew to colonial Cusco, tucked in the Andes, the capital of the Inca Empire. The highlight of Cusco was our visit to the city's Cathedral, a Dominican church and convent built upon land where the earlier Inca religion, which was dedicated to sun worship, had been built before it.

Then we moved on to a most wondrously impressive example of structural engineering—the ruins of Sacsayhuamán. Our guides told us the unbelievably amazing walls were constructed by the Inca with stones weighing up to 125 tons in this ancient fortress. This massive edifice, with its towering stone masonry, is something you have to see to believe is even possible. We were informed this was where battles later were fought between the Spanish and the Incas. We also visited "The Labyrinth," a limestone military construction of winding underground passages intricately carved with depictions of mystical and mysterious beings.

After returning to Cusco we checked into the Hotel Monastery, which was once known as the Seminary of San Antonio Abad—a fascinating place to stay that seemed to me to be as it was three hundred years ago. I don't wish to sound silly about this, but it was close to a religious experience.

After the monastery we were off to Machu Picchu aboard the auto-rail. We stayed at the Machu Picchu Sanctuary Lodge—the only lodging available up near the hilltop ruins. After getting settled, we went into the magical Sanctuary of Machu Picchu and were met by a Peruvian shaman who talked about the local legends of the moon, the constellations of the nighttime sky, and how the Incas incorporated these beliefs into their everyday life. Listening to this man touched me and, again, it nearly brought me to the sensation of spiritual experience.

At sunrise we could see an ethereal aura caused by the misty morning clouds surrounding the ruins—a spectacular sight. It gave us photo opportunities beyond imagination. We then had the chance to enjoy the incredible sights of Machu Picchu before all the usual crowds arrived. In that, our morning walk-about, I imagined how shocking this place must have been for Hiram Bingham, the archeologist who stumbled on the site in 1911. Breathtaking views everywhere one looked!

The next day we were off to the picturesque village of Pisac, which is known for its markets and as the place where villagers come from miles away to barter. We saw a lovely variety of pottery, ponchos, jewelry, and much more. While most people got busy shopping, though, I had more fun sneaking photographs of the photogenic locals.

We flew next to Ecuador's Quito, the second highest capital in the world, known worldwide for its culture as well as its ornate churches, cathedrals, and baroque architecture. The San Francisco Church, as one example, was awe-inspiring with its glittering interior, much of it embossed with

The terraced citadel of Machu Picchu was a highlight of our trip to Peru.

seven tons of gold. Then we drove up to El Panecillo hill, where we saw Quito's "Winged Virgin," which can be seen from almost anywhere in the city. This was very special for me, since I have a love of angels. Over the years, angels have popped up in much of my art.

Next we were off to the Galápagos Islands. We first flew to Guayaquil and then continued on to Baltra Island where we boarded the Eclipse—the boat we were on throughout our travels to many of the other islands. Once close to any particular island, we would negotiate our bodies

into a panga (an inflatable boat that held from eight to ten people).

Knowledgeable naturalists led our many excursions. On the Las Bachas Beach on Santa Cruz Island, our first guide pointed out several varieties of coastal birds, including a few pink flamingos. But there were also other critters: it was here we saw marine iguanas and Sally Lightfoot crabs. Following a subsequent wet landing on Santiago Island, we spotted fur seals, sea lions, more shore birds, and a couple of hawks. It was so much fun walking the beach so near to those fur seals and sea lions. After that stroll, we arrived at Bartolomé Island with its "Stairs of 375 Steps." Even though the name should have warned us, we pressed on, climbing so we might see the top of one of the most spectacular lookout points among the islands. And we made it and were rewarded with a splendid view of the bay.

The next morning we went to Genovesa Island with its panoramic view of Darwin Bay. Here again, the surroundings were filled with wildlife. We saw masked boobies, swallow-tailed gulls, and more sea lions. Genovesa was advertised as a great place for snorkeling, if that was your thing. We could see what fun it would be but, instead, we climbed back into the inflatable panga so that we could visit "Prince Philip's Steps." By the way, on occasions, while chugging toward various islands in our panga, we saw what seemed like thousands of stingrays. And then, too, we spotted sea turtles swimming beneath us. And sharks.

So when we got to "Prince Philip's Steps," we were met (perhaps not surprisingly) with another climb—this time it was up a steep cliff path to a forest of Palo Santo trees. There, we glimpsed hundreds of storm-petrels that flew along extensive lava fields as well as short-eared owls and tropical birds. And more boobies—we spotted both the blue- and red-footed boobies. And yes, the foot portion of their name is utterly and quite literally descriptive.

Although Machu Picchu is known for its location high in the Andes Mountains, its elevation was actually 3,000 feet lower than the Peruvian city of Cusco, at 11,152 feet above sea level, which we visited the day before.

Fernandina Island is the youngest of all the islands, home to some of the most unique species, including flightless cormorants and the Galápagos penguin. I loved the little penguin. We were quite surprised to see so many. This place also hosted one of the largest colonies of marine iguanas. I had not seen a lot of iguanas in my life. Which, of course, made this special. At Urbina Bay's beach on Isabela Island, the particular geology of that place meant we saw dried coral and sea organisms we hadn't seen on the other islands.

Next, we hopped yet another panga and rode through the mangrove forest of Elizabeth Bay off Isabela Island, There we got "up close and personal" with (well, at least we were "up close to") the Galápagos penguin. It was in Puerto Ayora on Santa Cruz, however, where we came upon what I had been so interested in visiting and experiencing when we planned this trip: the Charles Darwin Research Station, where efforts were being made to preserve the islands. And, too, it was there where we met the giant Galápagos tortoise, for this was a tortoise breeding and rearing center. I was glad to get a shot of Everett and me standing next to a big ol' bruiser of a tortoise named "Lonesome George."

On one of our last days, we headed to Punta Suarez. Again, we took a panga (by then, we'd gotten used to clambering into the things with something close to comparable ease). Punta Suarez was one of the most popular areas of the Galápagos, with wildlife that included Galápagos doves, finches, and, again, the masked and blue-footed boobies nesting along the trail. If that weren't enough, we watched incredible albatrosses make their clumsy wobble to the edge of the cliffs before launching their magnificent selves and taking wing.

It was also on Punta Suarez that we scrambled up yet another unforgiving cliff path. After negotiating the trail to the island's high point, however, we were treated to the spectacular view of what the guide described as the island's natural blowhole. This same guide had urged us along, skyward, on the huff-and-puff path, assuring us it would all

be worth it in the end. As the sight spread out below me, I mentally gave him all the credit he deserved. He was right.

To make a long story shorter than I wanted it to be, this was a great trip. It wasn't great just because Everett and I had the fun of scrambling up to the islands' breathtaking heights, of tromping near sea lions or penguins at the shorelines, and of riding the pangas (with guides and other travelers) as the boats slipped in and out of sheltered bays. And it wasn't great only because of the variety of beauteous birds, sea life, and many unique beasts pointed out to us. But, instead, it was great because of the great relief felt. I came away relieved that competent and caring naturalists (and scientists of all stripes) studied and protected the life there. Maybe the critters we saw that were listed as "endangered" would graduate out of that category.

And some day soon.

In Ecuador we made our second stop along the Equator (our first being on our trip to Kenya), top left, and in Peru we saw girls just like the one I later used as a subject for an oil painting, top right. Our visit to the Galapagos Islands afforded views of giant tortoises, bottom right, and iguana-covered beaches, bottom left.

Young Girl in Lima, Peru / Oil on Canvas / 12" x 12"

Learning from Fellow Artists

On many occasions I have copied the work of old masters and of other artists that I admire. None of them were ever painted to sell, but to learn from and to enjoy. Most of the copied paintings I have done are hanging in my home.

Copying masters has been something done by artists for centuries. The Louvre's copyist program has been in existence since the Louvre first opened in 1793, and there is a long line of artists waiting to study by copying the paintings of those who preceded them. I was very surprised to learn that Paul Cezanne and Pablo Picasso came to the Louvre to copy works of the old masters.

Through copying paintings you admire you can develop a bank of knowledge about color and techniques that you can draw upon when creating your own paintings. I have found this invaluable and a highly instructive practice.

Replica of *Girl with a Pearl Earing* by Johannes Vermeer / Oil on Canvas / 12" x 12"

Replica / Oil on Canvas / 16" x 20"

Replica / Oil on Canvas / 12" x 12"

Replica / Oil on Canvas / 11" x 14"

Replica / Oil on Canvas / 16" x 20"

Replica of *Leg Warmers* by Harvey Edwards / Oil on Canvas / 16" x 20"

Replica of *Repose (Dancer Resting)* by Richard E. Miller / Oil on Canvas / 24" x 24"

While visiting Japan, our wonderful tour guide, left, took us to view marvelous sites like the Golden Pavilion in Kyoto, facing page.

A Feast for the Senses

Over the years Everett and I have had many friends of Japanese origin. In 2005 we were delighted to have the chance to take a two-week tour of Japan. It was a great opportunity to learn more about that culture, and it also provided me with some superb photo opportunities. In particular I enjoyed the chance to snap shots of young children who were so very cute, polite, colorfully dressed, and (luckily for me) eager to pose.

Japan has a population of about 125 million people, which is more than three times the population of California, which has a similar amount of land mass. Despite this, amazingly, life in Japan seemed agreeably orderly.

After arriving, we spent a couple days touring Tokyo. We visited the Zojoji temple and Happo-en garden. We studied Japanese tea etiquette, table manners, and the proper use of chopsticks before a delightful evening cruise down the Sumida River. The highlight of Tokyo was a very early (5 a.m.!) visit to the Tsukiji Fish Market where we took in the incredible atmosphere of motorized carts, trucks, and (not so surprisingly) loads of people on foot hurrying about.

We then proceeded to Nikko and, later, to Hakone where we spent a night at a ryokan (a traditional Japanese inn). Along the way, we cruised on Lake Ashi and then visited the hot springs in the Owakudani Valley. The evening at the traditional ryokan was a special adventure that included us dressing in traditional garb and sitting on the floor for dinner. Perhaps that formal ceremony was more impressive to me than even the food! We then returned to sleep on our futon, which we found spread out on the tatami floor. Even at this early juncture, I found myself gently but fully immersed into the fine and exotic culture.

The delights didn't end there. We traveled to Nagoya to visit the Tokugawa Art Museum, which impressed me with its collection of beautiful and vibrant handscrolls depicting scenes from stories and Japanese history. Later we moved on to Takayama and Kyoto where we had thrilling whirlwind tours of the Kyoto Imperial Palace, the Nijo Castle, and finally the Kinkakkuji (Golden Pavilion)—this last stop was regarded as the most beautiful castle in Japan.

That evening we were entertained by geisha who played instruments, then sang and danced. The following day we took a local train to visit Himeji Castle, also known as the White Heron Castle. (This castle was also considered to be the most beautiful one in all of Japan—if I were to be the one giving out the prize I'd have been stymied.) However, Himeji Castle was designated a national treasure and a UNESCO World Heritage Site.

After this, we took an exhilarating bullet train trip to Hiroshima. Hiroshima was the emotional peak of our entire journey. We met with a Japanese survivor of the August 6, 1945, atomic bomb. In a sobering presentation, he gave his first-person account of having been in a Hiroshima suburb when the bomb fell. We spent much time at the Hiroshima Peace Memorial Park (near the bomb epicenter), which was built both to commemorate the terrifying bombing and to promote a peaceful future.

This trip to Japan complemented our earlier trip to China and helped us better understand the differences between the two Asian nations (as well as the conflicts between them). Of course, the beauty of each place greatly impacted me—as some of the photos

I've included here attest. I was at times utterly taken aback by the exquisiteness of design throughout the evocative temples. Or by the serenity of the unique garden layouts. Or by the colorful traditional garb we happened to see darling young people wearing.

All of it was inspiration for more paintings.

While touring, we spotted a number of young girls who were on their way to an event. I thought they looked so sweet in their traditional kimonos, so I photographed a couple of them separately and composed a single painting. Left: A souvenir I brought back from our trip to Japan.

Japanese Ceremony / Oil on Masonite / 12" x 12"

Printmaking, a Hands-On Pursuit

I've discovered over time that I have an intense interest not just in one but in many art forms. Printmaking has become one of them. I noticed a class being offered at an art center on Bainbridge Island, only a few blocks from my studio. So I registered. But long before doing so, I had already seen some impressive prints at the Seattle Art Museum that had intrigued me.

Also, over time, I had learned that Edgar Degas first encountered the monotype method of printmaking in the mid-1870s and felt the art form lent itself to improvisation and created spontaneous-seeming effects. Yet, he noted, it was a relatively simple process. He was apparently so enthralled with the process he was to make (over the years) some four hundred monotypes. Other artists such as Jasper Johns also embraced monotype printmaking; he said it produced wonderful and magical qualities.

These testimonials were enough to make me take heed and investigate. After I started the printmaking class here on the island, I almost at once decided that printmaking was an exciting way to create something unique and appealing. I saw there was a distinct element, a feel of originality to the resulting print. This was especially so for those forms where the process is unlikely to create any two images precisely alike. In those cases each result—no matter how many produced) is considered an original work.

I know of five different techniques used in printmaking but have used two. One is relief, a technique in which an impression is made by putting paint or ink on an object and running it through the press in order to transfer the image.

The other process is a monoprint/monotype, and I think of these processes as crosses between painting and printmaking. With monotype, you construct an image on a piece of Plexiglas or another surface using oil-based or water-soluble ink; that plate is affixed to a press, damp paper is placed on top, and the paper and plate are put though the press. Because of the nature of a monotype—the ink is transferred from the plate to the paper—only "one of a kind" prints are made.

A monoprint, however, involves the adding of some hand-painted image or color or hues on a previously made plate and then running the plate and paper through the press for a second time. With monotypes only one consistent impression can be made. With monoprints, changes in the images add many new desirous effects. Either way—monotype or monoprint—the process is exciting to me for it gives me the feeling there are no limits to what can be produced.

Whatever the printmaking method, I found that the paper used had an important impact on the quality of the final outcome. The range of available papers is so vast that it at first seemed to me it would be perpetual trial and error. I finally learned that some watercolor papers work well but came to ultimately decide that my favorite papers were handmade especially for printmaking. There were also choices to be made between the several brands of inks and paints for printmaking. Quite by accident, over time, I discovered that water-soluble oil paints mixed with a particular gel worked great. I was so excited when I discovered how the colors remained so bright.

Printmaking appeals to me because, like Jasper Johns put it long before me, the outcomes generated are wonderfully magical: there is a certain mystery folded into the end product. What will appear when you peel off the paper from the press? And although printmaking is many-layered in its stages and steps, oddly, doing print work is freeing for me. And it's so much fun. Printmaking is rewarding in another way. Because I now have a little press in my studio, I can relatively quickly create uniquely suited images for personalized prints for gift giving.

Curiosity / Monoprint / 13" x 13"

Guardian Angels / Monoprint / 13" x 13"

No Birds! / Monoprint / 12" x 16"

The hands-on process of monoprinting was exciting to learn. I'm also enamored with the layered effect the printing method produces.

Cruising New England

In October 2005, we were off on a New England cruise on the *Golden Princess*. We boarded the ship in New York. We'd heard so much about the striking Northeastern fall displays that we anticipated we'd have to carve out time on this trip to point at, gawk at, and "ooh" and "aah" over the foliage. However, it turned out much of our tour was spent on the backside of a minor tropical storm.

There were still great things to see. Our first port of call was Halifax, Nova Scotia, with one of the longest coastal boardwalks anywhere. The people of Halifax are historically known for having played a big part in the recovery effort for survivors and casualties from the *Titanic*. We dropped in to see (and were captivated by) the Maritime Museum of the Atlantic, which displayed photographs of those days. When many people think of Halifax they may well think of Peggy's Cove—the home of the most photographed lighthouse in the world. Yes, I took my fair share of pictures and did an oil painting of it first thing when I got home.

Our next port was Saint John, New Brunswick. We spent most of our time there visiting a picturesque fishing village called St. Andrew-by-the-Sea. Just off the coast there was a rich ecosystem of whales, dolphins, and seals. The whales were not interested in being seen when we showed up with our cameras in hand, but we did spot dolphins and seals. Nature had blessed this place with another amazing phenomenon: the Reversing Falls. At intervals, the force of the tide causes the river to change direction and flow upstream. We watched and marveled.

Early the next day we arrived at Bar Harbor, Maine. The town is on the northeast side of Mount Desert Island and is surrounded by the famous Acadia National Park. That time of year Bar Harbor is a superb, color-rich coastal glory. So, happily, Everett and I finally got an eyeful of New England's famous oranges and reds. From there, we also got to see further dazzling scenes on a drive up to Cadillac Mountain. The panorama from that height was great, but nothing's

perfect in life—for we were also surrounded by nasty deer flies giving us the once-over, obviously thinking we might be tasty.

Our next stop was Boston, where we walked the Freedom Trail (billed—according to every brochure, poster, and sandwich-board placard—as the most historic 2.5 miles in the United States). And, since history was soaked into so much of the brick and mortar of Boston, we also toured the Old North Church, Paul Revere's House, Bunker Hill, "Old Ironsides," and other historic musts that I now can't recall. We also hopped onto an educational bus tour to Lexington and Concord, where I imagined that if I strained my ears just so, I'd almost catch the echo of "the shot heard round the world."

We stopped at Newport, Rhode Island. Sightseeing was hampered, here again, by heavy rains; but, luckily that city is known for its mansions. We toured and enjoyed Rosecliff, The Elms, and Marble House. Then it was on to New York. We disembarked from our temporary vacation home—that is, our berth within the *Golden Princess*. We stayed at the Iroquois Hotel for a few nights so we might drop in on our favorite art museums and see several Broadway shows. While in New York City, we also did a sobering, emotional tour of the 9/11 site.

Life sometimes proves richer than anticipated. Everett and I had hopped a flight to the Northeast, frankly on something of a lark, with not too many concrete images in mind beyond the desire to relax and see why everyone raves about those states' autumn leaves. Sure, we did find delightful patches of bright leaves. But, too, everywhere we turned, history was bursting from the seams. And Mother Nature showed herself off in parklands, odd-acting river systems, and coastal waters crowded with sea life. And, finally, as so many of our trips provided, I was left with a bulging, messy stack of photographs I'd snapped while on tour. Somehow I knew they would be great inspiration for future paintings.

The cruise line that ferried us throughout New England in 2005 provided such a nice collection of photo prints that I probably didn't need to break out my camera—though of course I did. Bottom center: Our passes required to proceed through customs in Nova Scotia.

ENCAUSTICS

——

Encaustic painting had been something I'd wanted to do for a long time. Because I loved media that allowed me to be very hands on, I thought it would be a wonderful new skill to acquire. Fortunately, one day in the late 2000s I saw that a class was being offered at Oil and Water, the studio operated by instructor Richard Nelson, on how to do encaustic paintings. I jumped at the chance to sign up.

Encaustic painting, which uses pigment and beeswax, is a technique and form of art that actually predates oil painting. While the medium offers a lot of flexibility, the technique itself is quite tricky. You need to break the beeswax in chunks and melt in a hot palette, keeping the temperature below 220 degrees, ideally between 150 to 175 degrees.

Then you mix in damar resin and add your pigments. The hot encaustic color can be applied to absorbent surfaces like wood or used to burnish a photocopied image. If you want various effects, you can add paper or gilded metal leaf. I like drawing on rice paper with oil pastels and combining that with the encaustic work in collages.

The last step is to finish the painting by "burning in" with a heat gun or propane torch. It's delicate business—too much heat will melt it to nothing. It's necessary, though, in order to fuse the layers together and create a velvety finish.

You can then buff it to a shine. I love the final effect.

Working in encaustics is an interesting, hands-on process that I enjoyed mastering. The relationship between pigment, paper, wax, and heat produces an other-worldly effect I find compelling.

Angels Among Us / Encaustic / 8" x 10"

Although the technique of encaustic painting is used across all of these pieces, vastly different effects can result.

I'm Good / Encaustic / 5" x 7"

Bridge Over Troubled Water / Encaustic / 20" x 11"

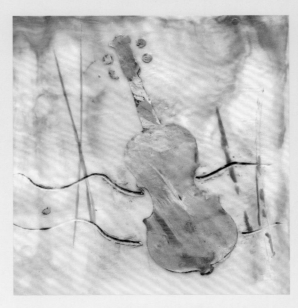

Archangels Unite / Encaustic / 11" x 14"

Going to School / Encaustic / 10" x 13"

Heavenly Music / Encaustic / 6" x 6"

What A Dreamer / Encaustic / 8" x 8"

Chihuly Space Needle / Encaustic / 6" x 6"

Maple and Ginko #1 / Encaustic / 8" x 10"

Maple and Ginko #2 / Encaustic / 8" x 10"

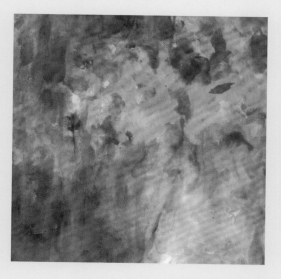

Flower Garden / Encaustic / 9" x 9"

It is a thrill whenever someone values my work enough to purchase it for their home. Teresa and Ken Schultz have purchased multiple pieces, including this pastoral scene, which they gave to their daughter.

Farm on Big Valley Road / Oil on Canvas / 16" x 20"

Reflections on Bernie

by Teresa Schultz

I first met Bernie DuBois about twenty years ago. My husband, Ken, did business with Everett. We would run into them here and there around the island and we enjoyed their acquaintance. We always looked forward to their Christmas card each year, for two reasons: Bernie's art and Everett's wit! Several times Bernie used her artwork depicting angels as the image for their cards. I loved that. I collect angels and have a room in my home dedicated to them.

In January 2011 I was diagnosed with triple negative breast cancer. Ken and I were walking through a corridor at Virginia Mason in Seattle and as we turned the corner, what caught my eye was one brick, among a whole wall of them, denoting a contribution made by Everett and Bernie DuBois. I said to Ken that when I got through all of this I wanted to get in touch with Bernie to visit with her, look at her art, and maybe even buy a piece because I love her angels so much.

My family came to celebrate my birthday when I was at the hospital. They brought cake and presents. There was one present that was quite large and in a big, flat box. I thought to myself, "What did they get me—a flat screen TV?"

I opened the box and pulled out a piece of Bernie's art called *Guardian Angels*. Beautiful, vibrant angels on canvas framed in gold. This took me by total surprise. I bawled my eyes out as soon as I saw the painting. It was one she had used on their Christmas cards one year and I greatly loved it. To think that my family was so sweet that they took note of what I had said and went and met with Bernie and picked out one of her paintings for me! This was one of the most touching, if not the most touching gift I had ever received.

I put it up in my hospital room window and admired it for the rest of the time I was there. When I got home, I wanted to hang the painting in a place where I would see it every day. I chose to hang it in my dressing area so I would see it every morning.

After a couple of years of owning the painting, I was looking at it one day and I was struck by the perfect symbolism of this painting and how it was truly meant for me: the main angel in the painting is a redhead. I am a natural redhead. This redheaded angel is wearing pink. Pink is the color that expresses moral support for women with breast cancer. This angel is holding a scepter of light. This is a symbol of power and enlightenment. I think if breast cancer gave me anything, it helped me focus on my blessings and on appreciation of life every single day and place my focus on what I want. This is my power. Bernie's painting has powerful meaning for me.

In recent years we have been lucky enough to spend a little more time with Everett and Bernie, occasionally enjoying each other's company for lunch, dinner, or an evening out. My experience of Bernie is that she is a fun-loving, joyful, spiritual woman. She is one of those people who truly pays attention to you and makes you feel important. I just love her style of painting. Her subjects seem to resonate with me.

A couple of years ago we met with Everett and Bernie at a winery where she was having an art show. I saw one of her paintings there that I couldn't stop thinking about called *Misty Morning*. When I first saw this painting it's like my whole being relaxed. Something about it is so serene and

Guardian Angels / Oil on Canvas / 24" x 18"

Misty Morning / Oil on Canvas / 11" x 14"

The first piece the Schultz family purchased from me was *Guardian Angels*, above, which Ken and his daughter gave to Teresa as a surprise birthday gift. Teresa then purchased *Misty Morning*, top right, for her home and *What a Find*, right.

What a Find / Oil on Canvas / 20" x 16"

I used *Guardian Angels* for one of my Christmas cards.

peaceful. It's a small painting on canvas that depicts almost exactly what I see out my window every day. I thought that maybe someday when I move away and no longer live where I have this view, Bernie's *Misty Morning* painting will be a little piece of that heaven reminding me of where I used to live.

At the same time I purchased *Misty Morning*, we were at Bernie's studio perusing her other paintings. That's when I first saw and purchased *What a Find*, which depicts a boy and girl finding treasures on a beach. This will be another fond reminder of my years of living at the beach.

When my husband, Ken; daughter, Stephanie; and son-in-law, Ryan were working with Bernie to select the *Guardian Angels* painting for me, Stephanie saw and fell in love with one of Bernie's paintings. It's of a two-story yellow house with sheep in the yard.

After a time, Steph told me about the painting and she thought maybe someday she would purchase it. When I was purchasing *Misty Morning*, I described the painting to Bernie and we figured out the painting Steph wanted. Ken

and I decided this painting would make the perfect gift to commemorate Steph's thirtieth birthday. She was surprised and thrilled with this gift! Coincidentally, Stephanie and Ryan moved into a two-story yellow house before receiving this painting. It's almost as if the sheep could be right out in their yard just like the painting.

We've acquired quite a bit of art, but it's just so much more personal with Bernie. She's just such a warm, friendly person. And I really connect to her art: I think serenity is the common theme when I think about each one of our paintings of hers. When you look at one of Bernie's paintings, it's like you're sort of this serene spectator on the world.

A Return to Africa

In May 2006 we were able to return to Africa, visiting South Africa and Botswana, as well as taking a brief trip to Zimbabwe to see Victoria Falls. After a one-night layover in London we arrived in Cape Town, South Africa.

Cape Town, established in 1652, was a stop for the ships of the Dutch East India Company, and it was beautiful.

We were fortunate to stay at the Cape Grace Hotel in the heart of Cape Town's Victoria and Alfred Waterfront, as it provided the perfect link between the elegance of the old city and the vibrancy of the waterfront.

The first thing you notice about Cape Town that is not highlighted in the travel brochures is the wind. It often is quite strong, and our attempt to ascend Table Mountain was delayed by a day. However, when we were able to take the aerial cableway, we had a spectacular ride up and took in a panoramic view of Cape Town from the top. The delay did prevent us from taking a ferry to Robben Island, the prison where Nelson Mandela, who was jailed for nearly thirty years for his opposition to Apartheid, spent eighteen years of his incarceration. We were sorry we missed it, as it was an important part of South African history.

We had an educational tour of Cape Town, including a visit to a "representative" family home. After that, we embarked on a half-day tour of the Cape Winelands, South Africa's premier wine-producing region. The tour included a visit to a private wine estate for a tour of its cellars. I found all this educational as I had not thought much about South Africa wines until then, but I was delighted by some of the wines we tried.

We spent the whole following day exploring the Cape Peninsula, traveling down the coast to the Cape of Good Hope Nature Reserve and Cape Point. Cape Point has a tram that takes you to a peak where you enjoy heart-stopping panoramic views. The most fascinating wildlife we encountered were the African penguins, a species unique to southern African waters. They are small—only about two feet tall and six pounds—and feed mostly on fish and squid. They were fun to observe.

The next day found us airborne to the Okavango Delta in Botswana. We ended up at Sanctuary Bainess Camp which is a luxurious tent camp overlooking the Boro River. It featured deluxe four-poster beds that could be rolled out under the stars. Due to the weather we chose not to sleep outside, but still did not escape adventure.

In the middle of the night Everett woke me up to report something had run over his arm, but a cursory search

On our second trip to Africa we visited South Africa, where I photographed Table Mountain, facing page, and Botswana, where we picnicked alongside elephants.

uncovered nothing. About an hour later, when I had a similar experience, the hunt was on. I then noticed a mouse run under my pillow. The chase ended with the little guy cornered and a towel placed over it. I opened the tent to release the mouse and, just as it jumped out of the towel, we heard a lion roar. We determined that we had encountered "The Mouse That Roared."

The next day we were enjoying lunch outside on the property when—bang!—something hit our table. We were so startled that it took us a few beats to realize that a monkey had landed on our table, snatched one of the bananas intended for us, and jumped back into a tree to feast on it.

The real adventure came the following day when we "walked with the elephants." A man originally from Oregon lives in the wilds with three elephants he had rescued as infants fifteen or twenty years earlier, when Botswana was thinning its elephant herds.

We were fortunate to be the only walkers that day. Our farm backgrounds instilled a combination of trust, respect, and caution that appeared to make the elephants comfortable around us. We were shown much about how they feed, walk, and think. We were encouraged to touch them and talk to them. In fact, my bonding with one of them almost led Everett to suspect a budding affair! We reached a picnic site where we ate while the elephants fed nearby. Afterward, we watched as the elephants enjoyed a swim in a nearby lagoon.

After more game viewing at Baines' Camp we moved to the Little Vumbura tent camp in a remote area of the Okavango. It was spectacular, situated in some of the largest and shadiest mangosteen forests imaginable. It was a great opportunity to see and enjoy animals drawn to the March-to-November flood plane.

Our next stop was Chief's Camp in the Moremi Game Reserve. The Moremi is renowned for its large prides of lions. There were many lions, leopards, elephants, buffalo, and even crocodiles. It was fun to watch the interaction around watering holes. We saw numerous sizable herds of Cape buffalo, but they were far from what Everett remembered

as his father's cattle herd. With deadly horns and a foul temperament they are the animal most feared by African natives. We also enjoyed a thrilling dugout canoe trip along the narrow Delta channels.

Continuing to move, we were off to Chobe Chilwero Lodge in Chobe National Park. The Chobe Game Reserve is 4,500 square miles and has an estimated elephant population of more than 60,000. In addition it has a large population of hippos, lions, crocodiles, and various bird species. On the river cruise we took, we were unsure of which bank to look at as both were teeming with wildlife.

It is difficult to choose a favorite experience, but it would be hard to top our visit to Victoria Falls, which concluded our trip. We arrived by car at the Victoria Falls Hotel. Opened in 1904, this 143-room colonial-style hotel provides views of the beautiful second gorge as well as the bridge that connects Zambia to Zimbabwe. The general mood in Zimbabwe was lower as economic conditions were very difficult, and this was reflected by the modest number of guests at the hotel.

We accompanied our guide down to the falls for our first look at this magnificent wonder. The rainbows that frequently crisis-cross the gorge during sunlight are more a painting than reality. The highlight of the Victoria Falls visit was a helicopter ride we took low over the falls and its gorges, giving us a breathtaking panoramic view of one of Africa's greatest spectacles.

The following morning we were off to Johannesburg to begin our journey home.

Our visit to South Africa and Botswana supplied a number of memorable experiences. We helicoptered above Victoria Falls, top and bottom right, and walked among elephants, top left. We enjoyed the stately accommodations of Victoria Falls Hotel, bottom left, and visited a representative home in one of Cape Town's underdeveloped townships, middle right.

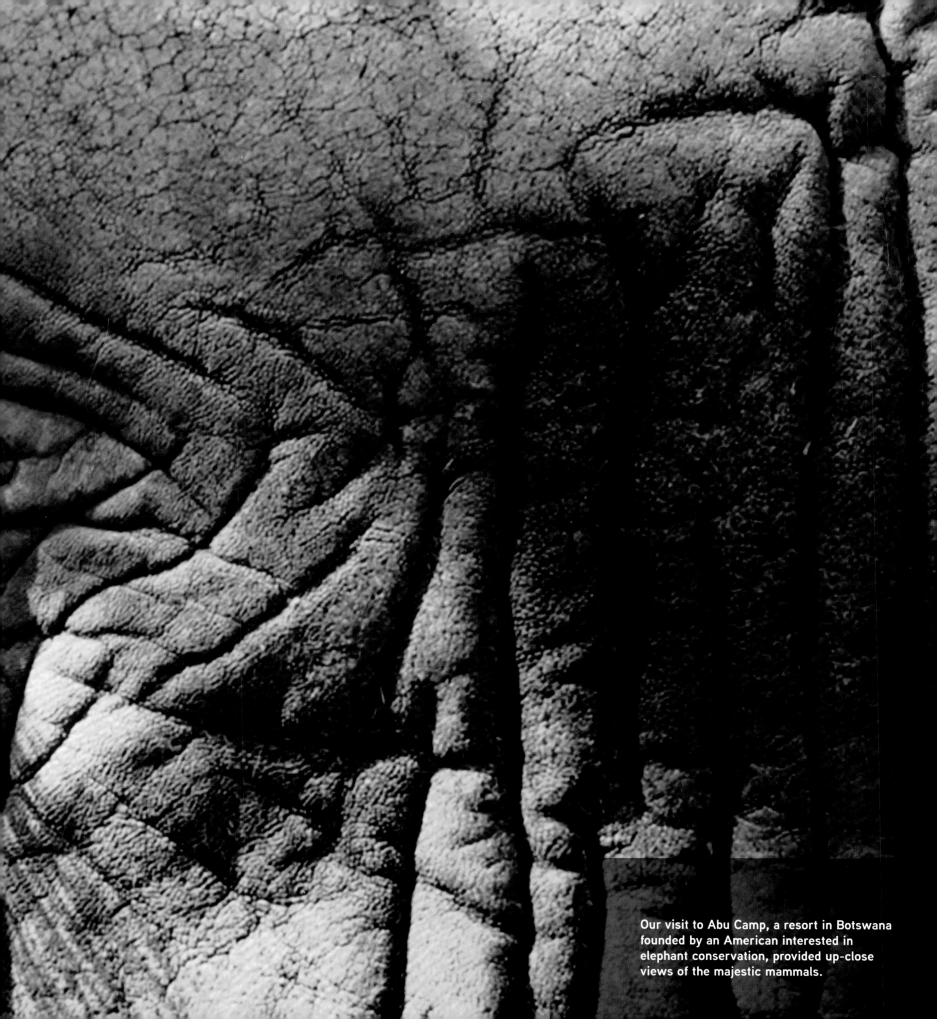

Our visit to Abu Camp, a resort in Botswana founded by an American interested in elephant conservation, provided up-close views of the majestic mammals.

Where Did They Go? / Oil on Canvas / 14" x 11"

Your Place or Mine / Oil on Canvas / 14" x 11"

Whooo Cares? / Oil on Canvas / 20" x 16"

Raven / Oil on Canvas / 9" x 9"

Birds and animals are enjoyable subject matter for me. Just as with my portraits of people, I seek to not only represent their physical nature but also capture a degree of their unique personality.

Artic Hare / Oil on Canvas / 16" x 20"

Another Beautiful Day / Oil on Canvas / 11" x 14"

That's Interesting / Oil on Canvas / 14" x 11"

Love it Here / Oil on Canvas / 11" x 14"

Athena / Oil on Canvas / 8" x 10"

Bernetta DuBois

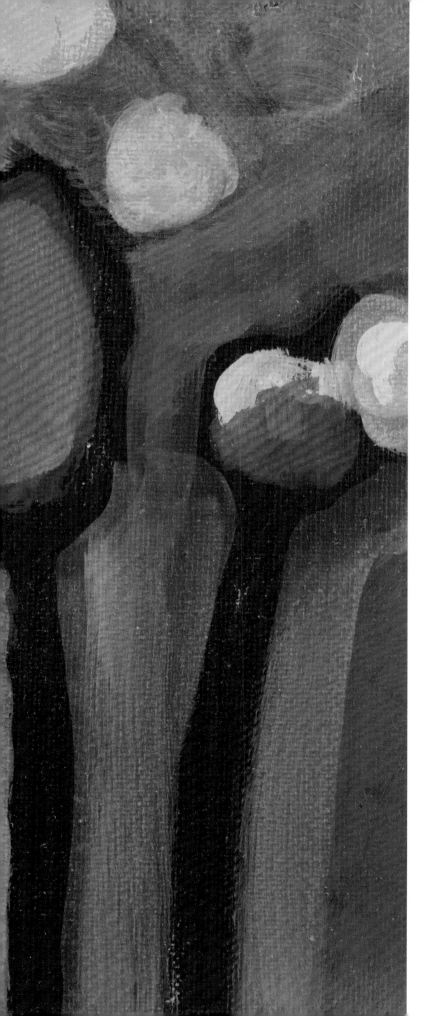

Fall Harvest / Acrylic on Canvas / 6" x 6"

The simplicity and beauty of
nature never fail to enchant me.
I painted these two pieces in
acrylic paint, which I use every
once in a while. Acrylic's fast-
drying properties, though, make
it less appealing to me than oil.

Joy of Spring Tulips / Oil on Canvas / 9" x 9"

Our visit to Egypt was extraordinary. To be in such close proximity to structures built nearly five thousand years ago was thrilling.

Walking Among Giants

In March of 2007 we revisited Africa for a third time, making a tour to Egypt called "Pharaohs & Pyramids." This was clearly a history lesson as opposed to the previous two wildlife tours. It was a wonderful trip under much calmer circumstances than those that were about to erupt in the Mideast.

We started the tour in Cairo by meeting the Egyptologist who would lead us on the tour.

Our first day was a visit to the Giza Plateau, where pyramids had been erected for pharaohs Cheops, Chephren, and Mycerinus 4,500 years ago. The Great Pyramid is the only survivor of the Seven Wonders of the Ancient World. We had a special chance to climb the narrow walkway to The Great Pyramid's King's Chamber, which was a bit more rigorous than I expected. This was followed by a ride on a camel with an attitude. Between the two, I managed to develop a serious limp the next day that was diagnosed as a stress fracture upon our return from the trip. I applied what Everett calls South Dakota medicine, known as "suck it up and walk it off" and was able to enjoy most of the rest of the trip.

While at the Great Pyramid we also were able to view the legendary Sphinx as well as visit the 141-foot-long funerary boat of King Cheops, which was only discovered in 1954 and subsequently reassembled. Nearby, we were also given special access to the excavations at the pyramid workers' own tombs.

It was seeing real archeologists at work and wondering how they could get so excited about finding a finger. (Now a skull—that's something else.) It's amazing the hours they can spend brushing dirt back and forth with what is the softest brush made on the planet.

The following morning (very early) we attended a private opening of the Egyptian Museum of Antiquities, home of the preeminent collection of ancient Egyptian artifacts. We marveled at golden treasures removed from the tomb of King Tutankhamun, as well as the fascinating Mummy Room—a fabulous collection that we were allowed to view close up and unobstructed before the large crowds arrived. Standing in front of the gold mask of King Tut was one of those moments I will never forget. For some strange reason, seeing that gave me the shivers. My thoughts were with Ed Hankey, my sculptor friend who sculpted King Tut as one of his first sculptures. I wished so much he could have been standing in front of that awesome sight.

Speaking of early, the next day we arose at 2 a.m. to catch a flight that got us to Abu Simbel at 7 a.m., allowing us to tour the Temple at Abu Simbel. The site houses two temples, the Great Temple of Ra-Harakhte, which is flanked by the four colossal statues of Ramses II, and the Temple of Hathor. It all was worth the early rise as, by noon, we were back at Aswan to board our boat for a week on the Nile. My sore leg rejoiced at the prospect of a week on a boat. What I didn't realize was that we would have a vigorous schedule of various land tours!

The first cruise day we visited the Aswan High Dam, followed by a motor boat ride to the stunning Philae Temple on the island of Agilka. That evening we had an "Egyptian Night" costume party, where people could dress in traditional Egyptian galabeyas. We participated, but beauty is in the eye of the beholder.

The following day we explored the extraordinary Temple of Horus at Edfu. We then cruised to Esna to explore the Greco-Roman Temple of Khnum at Esna. It sits about thirty feet below what is street level today because it had been long ago covered by silt from centuries of Nile flooding.

We then moved on to Luxor. We toured the East Bank of Luxor, starting at the Temple of Luxor. We then proceeded

to Karnak Temple. The great Hypostyle Hall has been likened to a forest of giant pillars because of the 134 columns that cover an area larger than that of Notre Dame Cathedral.

Probably the highlight of the Nile cruise was our visit to the Valley of the Kings and Valley of the Queens on the West Bank of Luxor. The tour included a visit to the tomb of Tutankhamun (King Tut). Also impressive was Hatshepsut Temple, the mortuary temple of Queen Hatshepsut, who was ancient Egypt's only female pharaoh. The day ended with a tour of the impressive Luxor Museum.

As we sailed toward the end of the cruise portion we moved off the beaten path to Nagaa Hammadi, passing by beautiful scenery to visit Abydos. Our final day had us visiting the Ptolemaic Temple of Goddess Hathor in Denderah. The main temple is almost in tact. We then returned to Cairo from Luxor.

Our final day was spent in Cairo with a visit to the hilltop Citadel, a medieval fortress built in the twelfth century.

We spent the remainder of the day preparing for our return to Seattle from Cairo.

So concluded our attention-grabbing history lesson. It not only taught us much, but fed our continued interest in Egypt and the Mideast as dramatic changes started to unfold.

Everett and I made the most of our trip, visiting King Tut's tomb, facing page left, and Abu Simbel, facing page right, and taking a ride on camels—a first for both of us.

Seeing the Great Sphinx of Giza—the magnificent lion-human figure—was a highlight of our trip to Egypt, our third visit to the African continent.

Eagle Harbor / Oil on Canvas / 30" x 15"

This painting, which I produced in 2008, has the nearly identical view that Everett and I would acquire with the purchase of our Winslow condo that same year.

Life on the Water

It wasn't until we moved to Bainbridge Island that I was blessed with the pleasure of boating with friends. Boats were never anything I really thought much about. I met Jan Herren when I took a watercolor class with her, and she and her husband Vern would take us out on their sailboat. We had some very special outings.

Never did I think I would be part of a sailboat race until Bob and Pat Lubowicki invited us to go boating with them. Unfortunately, the wind wasn't at our backs—no more need be said. It was one of those experiences that I will never forget because I learned that sailing is not for wimps.

When we moved back to Bainbridge Island in 1999, we had a waterfront home with a dock. We were probably one of the few people who had a dock and no boat. We learned early on that having friends with boats makes more sense than owning a boat.

Since we now live on the third floor of a condo, we have a view that overlooks the Eagle Harbor Marina and downtown Seattle. We now see and enjoy the sight of boats every day. The interesting part of this story is that when I did a painting of Eagle Harbor in 2008, little did I know that the view from my condo would be virtually this same scene.

Time to Sail / Oil on Canvas / 18" x 18"

Abandoned / Oil on Canvas / 20" x 16"

Settled In / Oil on Canvas / 14" x 11"

The marine activity of the waterfront communities around Puget Sound has been an endless source of interest for me.

Although our 2009 travels around the British Isles took place primarily by cruise ship, we bookended our vacation with visits to London, staying at the Mandarin Oriental Hyde Park.

Exploring the British Isles

By joining Everett on his business trips every once in a while over several years, we both got the chance to visit and explore wonderful London and the surrounding areas. We loved the place so much we developed a curiosity about the rest of the British Isles. In 2009, our chance came. We clambered aboard a twelve-day Princess Cruise of the Isles, departing from Southampton.

The first stop was in Saint Peter Port, Guernsey. Guernsey is the second largest of the Channel Islands and one of the sunniest places in the British Isles. We learned that Victor Hugo resided on the island from 1855 to 1870 and wrote *Les Misérables* while there. We did a walking tour of the town's shops and also visited Sausmarez Manor, which turned out to be a time capsule of Guernsey's changing fortunes over the past seven centuries.

We then sailed to Cork, Ireland's third largest city. We took a scenic bus tour through green, hilly countryside, the main destination being the 563-year-old Blarney Castle. I left it to Everett to join the crowded, winding walk up to the tower in order to give the famous Stone a smooch. He later confided, "Being from South Dakota, I now understand how Wall Drug can be considered a legitimate tourist attraction." Next was Dublin, a gracious and cosmopolitan capital city where we visited, among other sights, Saint Patrick's Cathedral, founded in 1190. Our final Irish stop was Belfast, in the north—a city that has experienced a bit of a renaissance since the 1994 ceasefire promised to end the decade-old troubles between Catholics and Protestants. However, there was edginess in the air. Perhaps what I sensed was still too much focus on the past and not enough looking toward a forgiving future.

We soon enough set sail for Liverpool, England, a heavily industrialized port famous for having given birth to The Beatles. We of course had to make a stop on Penny Lane—any sane person would. We left Liverpool for Glasgow, Scotland. People say it rains all the time in Seattle, but we

know better. Not sure we can say the same about Scotland. The highlight of our Glasgow stop was a motor coach trip through the countryside to tour Inveraray Castle. Built in 1746, it was the home of the Clan Campbell, which played a colorful part in Scottish history. We then cruised through what most would label a miserable fog but the Scots unapologetically called "the mists" to Invergordon, a place that has a deep-water anchorage. The ever-crafty Scots took advantage of this by constructing an important naval base, which remained there during the two world wars.

While in Scotland, we went to Loch Ness and joined the millions of visitors who've also never seen the Loch Ness Monster. Lunch introduced us to the Scottish culinary delight haggis. It's a "savory" mix of sheep's heart, liver, lungs, and spices traditionally encased in the same unfortunate animal's own stomach. Among tourists it (understandably) enjoys only modest popularity.

Our final stop in Scotland was in Edinburgh. We were informed it is known as the political, commercial, and cultural heart of Scotland. What I could readily see for myself was that it is a magnificently gracious place. We toured Edinburgh Castle, a historic fortress that dominates the Edinburgh skyline from every angle. In it we saw the Scottish Crown Jewels, Saint Margaret's Chapel, and the Great Hall of James IV and learned a wealth of tales about each. On that same afternoon, we toured the Royal Yacht *Britannia* (launched in 1954 and decommissioned in 1997). This was, for over forty years, the yachting home (and shouldn't we all have yachting homes?) to the Queen and Royal Family. The mostly original furnishings were luxurious on the one hand, but at the same time somehow modest and in good taste.

Our final stop before returning to Southampton was at Le Havre, in France. No other part of France holds more association for English-speaking visitors than Normandy, site of the landings of Allied Forces during WWII. Later, I won the rock-paper-scissors and so the two of us next spent some

At our visit to Buckingham Palace, we were able to view the changing of the guards, left, as well as see the impressive statues that make up the Queen Victoria Memorial, above and above left.

time touring Giverny, the home of Claude Monet just outside Paris. (Being an artist, of course, I carefully explained to Everett this was a truly religious experience and that I was disappointed he hadn't known that on his own!) The Monet house was filled with objects and art that had belonged to Monet, who lived in the place from 1883 to 1926. As his best-known works were his paintings of lily pads, Monet's gardens were impressively dotted with lilies in full splendor.

The cruise liner then returned us to South Hampton, and we made our way back to London. There we revisited the Churchill War Rooms (basement offices in Whitehall that served as the center of Britain's war effort). An impressive series of exhibits remain there. We also hopped onto some short cruises upon the Thames and even rode on the London Eye with its greatest of all views of London. (That said, the modernistic Eye sticks out like a sore thumb among the more picturesque, historical London monuments, like the nearby Globe Theatre.) Another highlight of our stay in the capital was seeing two outstanding London plays: the powerful *War Horse* at the New London Theatre and a good production of *Billy Elliot*.

Everett and I had previously dipped our cups in the punch bowl that was London and only knew that we wanted to see more of England. That's what had gotten us on that cruise. And, as with most travel, I don't think we entirely grasped that our experience was more than the quenching of curiosity. Upon returning to Seattle, and after we'd slumped into our easy chairs and thumbed through our snapshots and souvenirs, we realized the trip had served us up tidbits about the people, their travails, their art, theater, and history. When I think back on it I still get a lingering impression of the Scots' pride of accomplishment. I recall and still feel that conflict that I believed sadly endured within the Irish. And, more happily, I also sense how sure-footed most Londoners felt about the cultural contributions they'd made over the centuries around the globe.

In these upbeat ways, this trip seeped into my psyche.

Going Public

I've always liked creating art, and I even like talking about my art but—even though it is pleasing to have someone want to buy my art and hang it in their home—getting to that point is not necessarily my favorite part. Marketing myself is not my thing.

Despite my initial reluctance, I am proud to have had six solo shows on Bainbridge Island and in Poulsbo.

It was while working with artist Julann Campbell that I had my first showing at Wing Point Golf and Country Club. Everett and I were social members at the club, and Katy Goldsberry who was the manager at Wing Point, would always ask, "Oh, Bernie, what are you working on? May I see your latest painting?" As we talked about my art o ver time, she finally said, "Bernie, you have got to have a show here." At first I said I wasn't sure I could do it, but eventually I agreed.

I began preparing for the summer 2010 show in May. I painted a self-portrait especially for the show and set about deciding what other works I would include.

I don't think one really realizes the work involved in putting on a solo show. I put a lot of energy into it: I made cards with my name and a little about me; I had to name every work and make nametags for them; and I had to price everything. I also had to frame all of the pictures, which was a huge amount of work and a bit of an investment. Wes and Andrea of Roby King Galleries came to my studio and helped me figure out how to price my pieces. They also helped me frame many of the forty-four pieces that would go on display throughout Wing Point's lobby, restaurant, and lounge.

I'm very happy I did it, though. Everett was an absolute precious angel. He wanted everyone in the world—all of our friends and everybody else—to see it. We had friends come over from Seattle and took them to dinner at the club so they got to see it. They all loved my work and enjoyed seeing it displayed. I felt it was all very much worth every bit of that energy I put into it to see my friends so pleased and supportive.

I sold a few monoprints, two large oil paintings, and some encaustics at that show. But what really made that first Wing Point show worth the investment was the appreciation I felt from Everett for my art. It was all that I'd always hoped for from him.

My show lasted for six weeks. The sweet staff at Wing Point didn't want me to take my pieces down, and said how sad it was when I eventually did. I showed my work again at Wing Point in 2014—a smaller show, just sixteen pieces that time, but also one that was up for a couple months, and also one for which I painted a special self-portrait.

Eleven Winery hosted three of my solo shows—on Bainbridge in May 2011 and June 2012, and in Poulsbo in December 2012. It was wonderful to visit with friends and speak to members of the community about my work.

On September 13, 2013, Everett and I hosted a reception for the opening of my month-long solo show at Roosters Café, in their original location on Bjune Drive. We served drinks, hors d'oeuvres, and dessert, and had a wonderful time visiting with all the friends who showed up to support me.

In addition to these solo shows, I've also been honored to participate in two group shows in Houston since we left Texas. The first was in December 2011, when I showed two paintings at the Jung Center in the Houston Art Museum district. The second was a showing of five paintings I did in April and May of 2015 at the Brazosport Center for Arts & Sciences in Clute, Texas. It was so nice to be included along with my friends from Willy Wang's workshop—especially since more than a decade had passed since we'd lived there.

BERNETTA (Bernie) DUBOIS

Putting together shows is far more work than people realize. However, the chance to see my work hanging en masse in a public venue is truly exciting—making it worth the extra effort.

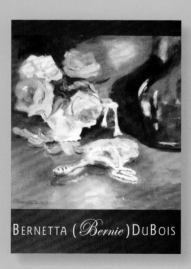

BERNETTA (Bernie) DUBOIS

Summer Feast / Oil on Canvas / 9" x 9"

WING POINT GOLF & COUNTRY CLUB
Bainbridge Island, Washington

I produced two shows for Wing Point, where Everett and I are members. Not only was it a thrill to sell a number of paintings and have so many friends and family view my work—in particular my brother, James, bottom right on facing page—but producing a long-running solo show gave me a measure of confidence I didn't previously possess.

Self Portrait / Oil on Canvas / 10" x 16"

Bernie DuBois

bernie@bernieonmadison.com

Over the years, my interest in art has evolved into my passion. I've worked in pottery, clay sculpture, and produced lost wax bronze sculptures. Presently I'm concentrating on oil painting, printmaking and encaustic.

Art serves as a way to express who I really am and touches my soul. I call it "soulful activity". I try my life with love and optimism. I hope that qualities show through in my work.

Front: Flowers & Pearls 18x18 Oil   Back: Self Portrait 16x10 Oil,   Angels Among us 10x8 Encaustic

Self Portrait / Oil on Masonite / 11" x 17"

BARGAIN BOUTIQUE
Bainbridge Island, Washington

My show at the sweet little thrift store benefitted Seattle Children's Hospital. It was another honor to see my work displayed in public, and the dedicated, mostly volunteer staff could not have been more gracious.

Delicate Balance / Oil on Canvas / 20" x 16"

BRAZOSPORT CENTER
Clute, Texas

Another opportunity to show with my Houston friends came in 2015. This time, I sent five pieces to be displayed, including *Delicate Balance*, above. It was wonderful to be reunited with the Willy Wang workshop group.

Waiting to Sail / Oil on Canvas / 36" x 24"

ELEVEN WINERY SHOWS
Bainbridge Island and Poulsbo, Washington

The owners of Eleven Winery agreed to host three of my shows over the years. The conviviality of these events made them particularly enjoyable, and it was a privilege to display and sell many paintings at these events.

THE JUNG CENTER
Houston, Texas

I was honored by the invitation to show two paintings alongside works produced by my old friends and former fellow students of Willy Wang's workshop in 2011. I missed my dear friends in Houston, so this show made it feel like old times.

20th ANNIVERSARY
WILLY WANG WORKSHOP

LIVING PORTRAITS
FACE • FORM • FIGURE

This exhibition is dedicated to Willy Wang

Jung Center of Houston, December 1-21, 2011

Rainy Day in Seattle / Oil on Canvas / 12" x 9"

ROOSTER'S CAFÉ
Bainbridge Island, Washington

The highlight of my show at Rooster's Café was the fun reception Everett and I hosted for friends. I also felt my paintings showed beautifully in the well-lighted space. Far right: Three of the pieces that sold at this show.

Wine * Beer * Soft drinks
with a lovely assortment of hors d'oeuvres
and dessert will be provided.

Date: Friday, September 13
Time: 6 pm - 8 pm

Location: Roosters Cafe
123 Bjune Way
Bainbridge Island, Wa

Please R.S.V.P. by September 1st
Email: bdubois@q.com
Phone: 842-5496

You Think So / Oil on Canvas / 9" x 12"

Bainbridge Coyote / Oil on Canvas / 12" x 12"

A Classic Journey

In September 2011, for a thirty-fifth anniversary present to ourselves, Everett and I took a great tour of Rome, the French Riviera, Paris, and London.

We started our trip in Rome, where we checked into a delightful hotel room at the top of the Spanish Steps. From there, we met with a guided tour that shuffled us through the Vatican Museum, Saint Peter's Basilica, and Saint Peter's Square. And then, of course, they escorted us into the Sistine Chapel. Nearly teary and craning my neck to gaze up and around us at Michelangelo's monumental work, I had a hard time folding my mind around the notion that any artist would even sign on for a project of such scope.

The next day a prearranged guide met us at our hotel and took us to the famous Forum and Colosseum. While there, we learned some details about the history and meaning of each site as we walked around the massive constructions. Those Romans—such engineers extraordinaire! I hadn't known before this that a few of those clever devils had even put an elevator into the Colosseum! While our guide's patter filtered into my ears, I imagined toga-wearing, sandal-clad ancients filing past, going about their business.

On the way back to the hotel, we stopped at the Trevi Fountain (of Sinatra song fame). At the last minute I decided to toss my own "three coins" into the fountain and sacrifice the afternoon cappuccino. Before leaving Rome we visited the Capitoline Museums and the Galleria Borghese, and we took in the rarified air of the massively impressive Pantheon built in 118 AD.

For what it's worth, here's my "take-away" on Rome: Rome is the definition of beauty. The architecture, Michelangelo's contributions, the life-sized Bernini sculptures on the Colonnade of Saint Peter's Square at the Vatican—these are only a cluster of examples.

Everett and I returned to Europe in 2011, this time focusing our travels on Rome, Nice, and Paris. We stood at the Arch of Titus in Rome, facing page, and visited the Louvre, above left, as well as the Eiffel Tower, above.

Our stay at the Hotel Regina in Paris, above, put us right next to the Louvre, which was visible from our balcony, above left. Our travels took us to the Roman Colosseum, far left; the Musée Rodin, left; and the Vatican, facing page.

Then throw in the overpowering scale of things, the incalculable number of art pieces, the opulence of even some of the streets and plazas and what you've got is, well, beauty. To put it another way, I can't separate out whether (artistically speaking) I was stimulated by any one painting, building, or sculpture or whether I was swept up in the famous capital as an overall experience.

From Rome we flew to Nice to spend three nights at the Hotel Château Eza in the hilltop village of Èze. There were no motorized vehicles to the hotel so we walked the last quarter mile. It was worth it, for we then merrily explored Èze's shops, sampled lip-smacking food, and sauntered around on quaint walkways. My breath was taken away by yet another treasure that this part of the world freely offers— astounding vistas. Looking out from the vantage point of our room's deck, for instance, could inspire any painter worth their salt. Laid out before us like a buffet was a spectacular view of the Mediterranean. Oh, and did I mention we took all of it in from inside a steaming hot tub? This was an unforgettable trip.

In time, we moved on, traveling a scenic train route through striking French countryside. We had four nights scheduled in a room at our Paris hotel (The Regina) with its view of the iconic Eiffel Tower. The hotel had easy access to the Louvre and to the Musée d'Orsay. Degas' several ballet scenes shown at the Musée d'Orsay were magnificent. (I love ballet as you can see from some of my work. Degas' images catch the heart and soul of the dance.)

However, it was the Musée Rodin that was most special to me while in Paris. I categorize Rodin's expressive work as the sheerest of brilliance. Whenever I sculpt, smilingly (and only half-kiddingly), I wonder what incantations might I invoke to best channel the heavily bearded Frenchman so he might flow into my brain, arms, and hands.

We were, all too soon, off to catch the train through the Chunnel to London, one of my favorites. I'd previously joined Everett on many of his London business trips and therefore have visited most of this stately capital's major museums and

attractions. And I didn't mind visiting the National Portrait Gallery and other small but probably equally famous museums like Sir John Soane's and the Wallace Collection. Great stuff was on view.

We made it back home from this fabulous whirlwind anniversary tour in one piece. Inwardly, I felt reinvigorated— as happens when our travels take us to diverse cultures. But it was Europe's grand historical perspective that brought me a greater degree of joy. This is because so many cities and rural settings "over there" are fine (and paintable or photographable) vistas in themselves. But like arty folk everywhere, I suppose, I find the experience of viewing Europe's unrivaled collections of past masters utterly soul-quenching.

From the ceiling of the Sistine Chapel, above, to the sculpture in the Louvre's Tuileries Gardens, facing page, this trip was truly an artist's delight.

BAINBRIDGE ISLAND BERRIES

Moira McDonough and I had terrific fun concocting our "Grand Marshall" frog for the Bainbridge Island Downtown Association. Placed in front of the Bainbridge Island Historical Museum initially, it was auctioned off and now resides in Winslow Mall.

Reflections on Bernie

by Moira McDonough

Bernie's and my paths crossed at an estate sale she was having when she moved into their condo in Winslow. Sometimes you have a connection with someone. I felt like I had known her all my life when we were talking. She gave me several potted plants, and we have been friends ever since.

I am a graphic artist and as I learned about the different art that Bernie has produced and the fact that she was still committed to ongoing education, I was just in awe. She became a kind of mentor to me, as well as a friend. We would attend shows at BIMA, talk about our respective projects, and trade plants from our gardens.

I was deeply touched when, in 2013, Bernie asked me to "co-design" a large frog sculpture that she and Everett had sponsored for a fundraiser put on by the Bainbridge Island Downtown Association. Since the frog was intended for the Bainbridge Island Historical Museum, we settled on a design that placed the frog atop a strawberry and named it the "Grand Marshall" in honor of the Marshall strawberry grown on the island before World War II and the fact that we dressed our frog as a dignitary. Bernie's unending creativity and abundance of experience in different mediums helped us to execute a very whimsical, colorful frog, which still stands proudly in the downtown center of Bainbridge Island.

Bernie was very hands-on with the frog project, and bought all the materials we used to produce it. Almost two months after it was installed on the historical society's grounds, it was vandalized and part of the frog's hind leg was chipped. Bernie was very devastated because it's a work of art. We repaired it with putty and the same sign paint we used to decorate the frog, and I think Bernie was pleased that we were able to recover it as well as we did.

It was a real privilege having worked with her on this project and experiencing the love and generosity she expresses daily in all her artwork. I call her an "Earth Angel" because she touches so many lives in our community. Bernie is an incredibly generous woman. If you see her going around downtown or through our local grocery store, the number of people she knows is amazing. Every time you see her, it's, "Honey." Everyone's her honey. She just has a warmth about her that makes people feel very loved by her. She's very authentic

I am honored and blessed to have Bernie in my life.

Harbor View / Oil on Canvas / 20" x 16"

Harborside / Oil on Canvas / 20" x 16"

Be Our Guest!

Rise & Shine

HOUSING RESOURCES BOARD
SECOND ANNUAL FUNDRAISING BREAKFAST

Become a Hou...

COME ONE, COME ALL!
BAINBRIDGE PERFORMING ARTS'
ONE STARRY NIGHT
2015

ONE STARRY NIGHT
BPA
JANUARY 25, 2014

2. HARBOR VIEW OIL PAINTING

Painted by beloved friend of BPA and well-known local artist Bernetta Dubois, "Harbor View" perfectly captures the color and light of Eagle Harbor. This professionally framed 20 x 16 oil on canvas is one of a kind; whether you love sailing, the waters of Puget Sound, or just fine art, this beautiful piece is bound to anchor your collection.

Thank you to our donor,
Bernie Dubois
Value: $750

I have been honored to be asked to donate works of art to various local nonprofits through the years, usually for use in charity auctions. Here, an array of marketing materials for these events are shown, as well as two pieces auctioned at the 2014 and 2015 Bainbridge Performing Arts gala.

COLLAGE

—

With collage, you create a work of art by pasting disparate, somewhat flat items—like photograph fragments, newspaper clippings, coins, and theater tickets (almost anything, really)—onto a single surface. I guess I would have to say it is the layering of thoughts and ideas as well as paper, fabric, glue, and paint.

Although adopted by renowned artists like Pablo Picasso and Georges Braque, many people consider collage more of a craft than an art. However, it can be formal and as expressive as painting. The techniques we know as collage today were no doubt known by other names in the distant past.

Collage has been a dynamic, as well as exciting, medium for me as an artist. I love it because it provides a second life for found papers and objects. Another way of putting it is that it brings order out of chaos. Once I get an idea of what I want to accomplish with a certain subject matter it seems as though a relentless search is on until I get everything I need. For some unknown reason it brings the child out in me—it's like a treasure hunt.

Collage provides me with an opportunity to make gifts that can be personalized by including such details as names, pets, and things the recipients are interested in and appreciate. I must admit that I do love making collages for family and friends, and it is also a great way for me to let them know they are loved.

There are many ways of describing collage, but I love what art critic Donald B. Kuspit said: "Collage makes poetry with the prosaic fragments of dailiness."

Collage allows me to bring together
several mediums into one piece. Here,
I combined photographs taken on
one of our trips to Africa with found
objects and handmade paper.

Kenya / Collage / 12" x 16"

Heavenly Peace / Collage / 8" x 6"

Angels have been a common
theme of the collages I've
produced, and they often end
up gracing the covers of my
Christmas cards.

Here to Help / Collage / 10" x 10"

Guardian Angels / Collage / 18" x 18"

The Guardian Angels / Collage / 12" x 12"

Eleven Winery #1 / Collage / 9" x 9"

Eleven Winery #2 / Collage / 9" x 9"

Eleven Winery #3 / Collage / 9" x 9"

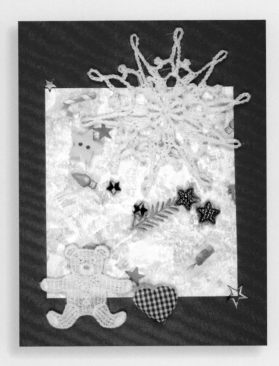

I often use photos in my card-making process—these are cards I make for all sorts of occasions and then later send to family and friends. Sometimes photos are used as part of a collage that turns into the card itself. At other times I merely include a print of one of my pictures to be placed within the fold of a card. Always I hope that these photos will be treasured. If I can't be right there in person with a friend or family member, then sending one of these cards—one I've created using a unique photo or that includes one or many special pictures within it—is the same as sending a love note. If it's a special image of them or of something or someone dear to their heart, my feeling is that it stands in for a great big hug from me.

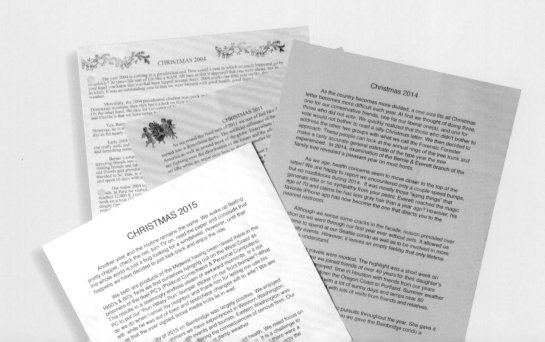

Frog Rock, Bainbridge Island, WA

My life with Everett has truly been a
blessed adventure—not only in terms of
our travels together but also the journey
in uncovering my love for producing art,
which Everett has supported. Facing page:
Everett's favorite painting.

Reflections on Bernie

by Everett DuBois

Life with Bernie has been an adventure. Together we've lived in places—and visited many more—that are a far cry from where we both grew up. Along the way, Bernie and I have developed our shared appreciation for the arts, and Bernie has developed into an accomplished artist in her own right.

We were both raised on farms in the Midwest and attended one-room schools for our primary educations. Our parents had similar values based in hard work and families, though my childhood was a bit more comfortable than Bernie's. Mine was sort of an "Ozzie and Harriet" family, as I had a brother five years older. Although my father had mid-life health issues, we always felt very secure. Bernie had five sisters and a brother during the Depression, an economic time when it was sometimes a struggle to provide even life's minimum necessities to large families. All her family members had to do their share of strenuous chores to survive. Her parents were from strict German stock and believed in hard work, which they expected to be done without complaint and without their handing out compliments for the efforts. This resulted in a lot of competition for attention among the siblings, which was really a competition for self-esteem.

I believe we all have a search for self-esteem in our lives. Perhaps I had found mine in business. Bernie eventually found hers in art.

Early on in our relationship, Bernie did not consider herself an artist, nor did she spend much time on hands-on art activities like she has the past three decades. It was clear to me, though, that she had an artistic interest. She had a flare for design, and she certainly showed that in the places we lived. Let's say she upgraded my decorating. She could look at a blank space, visualize what it could be like, and then create it. I'm exactly the opposite: I can look at something and tell you if I like it or not, but I can't say, "Let me put that together," like Bernie can.

Bernie and I were both forced to overcome physical obstacles in our early years and, to an extent, for the remainder of our lives. As we got to know each other better, it became obvious that, in addition to common backgrounds, we also shared many similar character traits. Among them were a general curiosity about all things, a sense of adventure, and a determination to complete what we set out to achieve.

Due to our backgrounds, neither of us had had much exposure to culture or travel. This left us a free slate to pursue interests in everything, from rodeos and baseball to ballet and opera. The following years gave us time to travel and further pursue our curiosities.

In 1981, that sense of adventure and determination that we shared was put to a real test. We were offered the chance to transfer to Seattle from Saint Paul. Although we each had previously migrated to Minnesota, we were nonetheless

Replica of *Angela* / Oil on Canvas / 16" x 2

Over the course of four decades of marriage, Everett and I have been true partners. Ours is a love for the ages.

Peace on Earth

Midwesterners, and the West Coast represented a dramatic change.

We settled on Bainbridge Island. While I was busy at work with people I already knew, Bernie had a lot to adjust to in the new surroundings. Looking back on it, that was probably emotionally one of the more difficult periods of her life because not only was she separated from her family at a time when both of her parents passed away, but she was somewhat isolated on Bainbridge. She is the oster girl for "Midwest Friendly" and yet, without children or friends available, she felt lonely among the more reserved ens of Bainbridge. It was a difficult time for her.

Bernie channeled her energy into her longtime interest She started modestly enough by working on ceramics newfound instructor and friend, Karen Wilson. Karen is rful woman. I think she helped Bernie more than she by initiating her into mainstream Bainbridge through aderie her classes offered and also getting Bernie's es flowing again.

Bernie excelled at ceramics. She's very task oriented and an amazingly fast painter. We all are contradictions, but Bernie's a particular contradiction of patience and impatience. She's got to be patient to be an artist but she's impatient to be done with the work. I think that impatience is what drove her sense of adventure to start looking for a different means of making a personal art statement. She found it at Olympic College in Bremerton, where she began taking metal sculpture classes. She proved to be a natural at sculpting and produced some very nice bronze pieces using the lost wax method. One of these was her father's memoir piece, of which prominent local fisherman Bruce Gore said, "If you ever want to sell that, come right over and name your price." I think that's probably when Bernie got her first dose of confidence about her art.

In 1989 and 1990, Bernie spent much of her time overseeing the building of our new house on Bainbridge. It turned out well, but in 1993, we faced the spirit of adventure once again when I learned there was an opening at work that called for a move to Houston. Bernie was ready for a change and so, in October 1993, we were off to Texas.

Houston and Texas greatly exceeded both our expectations. Houston is a great commercial city and was well suited to my company and skill set. It is also a friendly, open city—Texas is essentially South Dakota on steroids— where Bernie could, and did, quickly make friends. She was fortunate to connect with outstanding artists and sculptors. For instance, she was "adopted" by a community of Chinese artists led by Willy Wang, an internationally known artist. She also connected with a gifted Houston sculptor, Ed Hankey. She remains good friends with Ed and Willy as well as many of her Chinese friends, and we regularly visit each of them when in Houston.

Bernie was also fortunate to befriend Cookie Joe, a Chinese American who was a ballerina and also ran a ballet school. Cookie was very generous in sharing her knowledge of ballet with Bernie, which included letting Bernie watch and photograph her students as they performed. This was reinforcement for Bernie's longtime interest in that dance style. It motivated her to focus many paintings and sculptures on the subject of ballet. The combination of getting to know Houston's talented artists and making other good friends there meant this was one of the happiest times of Bernie's life. And it stimulated her to become even more immersed in her art going forward.

Texas was a great adventure for the both of us, as it was a big buffet of all forms of culture and sports. We'd been able to explore the vast diversity of that state in various road trips (to Dallas, Austin, San Antonio, El Paso, and points beyond). Before retirement, Bernie had been able to join me for annual business trips to London and Bermuda. (I think the London art museum visits were a great inspiration to her.) During our time in Houston and then also in our later retirement years in Seattle, we continued to travel. For example, we took many trips to New York City. Bernie was able to visit all the major museums there, too—multiple times, seeing many special exhibits.

In 1999, I had the opportunity to retire, and all the stars seemed in alignment to do so. It meant that the two of us might pursue many things that time had not previously allowed us to do. It was difficult to leave all our friends in Houston, but now that we were retired, the undesirable Texas weather tipped the scales. In November of 1999, although it was a bit of a surprise to both of us, after numerous visits, we found our way back to Bainbridge Island.

During our second stint on Bainbridge, Bernie again connected with the community through her art. She took classes from Julann Campbell, who was a kind of missing link for Bernie in terms of elevating her oil painting. Plus Julann brought Bernie into a rather eclectic group of people who painted together. Several of them were also very talented,

and they helped each other by being a very honest group of critics. It drove Bernie to do more and better work.

Bernie gained self-confidence by getting a private space for a studio of her own in 2010. However, the greatest boost to Bernie's self-confidence came from her first show at Wing Point Golf & Country Club. Bernie's a very social person so everybody knows her and everybody gets a hug. The management at Wing Point knew she was an artist and asked if she wanted to do a show, so she dug out about forty-five different pieces. It was one of their better shows. It provided the credibility that Bernie didn't feel she had before that. It is said that this doesn't matter, but there's nothing that pleases an artist more than having a stranger buy his or her work. And that was the case for Bernie. I think people were always convinced she was a better artist than she thought she was. As enough people told her she was good, she started to accept it and, over time, she came to believe more in herself.

The Wing Point show was also the turning point for me in recognizing just what an accomplished artist Bernie had become. I was proud of what she had done and wanted to have people see it, so I was glad to take many of our friends out to dinner to view the show. Although I think I had expressed appreciation for Bernie's work before this, I never took her art as seriously as I should have until then, when I realized how good it was and what she was building. There's a little bit of guilt that I didn't give her the reinforcement that she may have needed, that she never got as a younger person.

I'm certainly proud of her art. I'm proud of her gaining the self-esteem where she needed it the most. I am also proud that Bernie stood her ground and refused to sell her works she valued most. Therefore, our condos are filled with quality and personal works of art.

I think there are quite a few good sculptors, there are quite a few good encaustics people, and there are quite a few good oil painters. But, I'm not really aware of anybody who can do all those quite as well as Bernie can.

GALLERY

Mayume #1 / Oil on Canvas / 12" x 12"

Mayume #2 / Oil on Canvas / 12" x 12"

Mayume #3 / Oil on Canvas / 12" x 12"

Mayume #4 / Oil on Canvas / 12" x 12"

Rachel / Oil on Canvas / 20" x 24"

View on Big Valley Road / Oil on Canvas / 20" x 16"

Ballet at its Finest / Oil on Canvas / 14" x 11"

Great Performance / Oil on Canvas / 20" x 16"

Maria / Bronze / 16" tall

Contemplation / Hydrostone / 21" tall

Leaf #1 / Durasculpt / 25" x 21"

Leaf #2 / Durasculpt / 31" x 28"

Time to Play / Oil on Canvas / 14" x 11"

I Know That / Oil on Masonite / 12" x 16"

Loving Moral Support / Oil on Canvas / 16" x 20"

Day Spa / Oil on Canvas / 16" x 20"

Tea Time / Oil on Masonite / 24" x 24"

Geranium Wine / Oil on Canvas / 18" x 18"

Sarah's Picture / Oil on Canvas / 24" x 24"

Lillies / Oil on Canvas / 20" x 16"

Garden House in Sequim / Oil on Canvas / 12" x 9"

Julann's / Oil on Canvas / 12" x 16"

Pitchers / Oil on Canvas / 24" x 20"

Grandma's Birdhouse / Oil on Masonite / 28" x 30"

Sunset / Oil on Canvas / 20" x 16"

Seagull Enjoying the Day / Oil on Canvas / 20" x 16"

Lavender Fields in Sequim / Oil on Canvas / 20" x 16"

Eagle Harbor Marina / Oil on Canvas / 20" x 16"

Sisters / Oil on Canvas / 20" x 16"

Summer Home / Oil on Canvas / 20" x 16"

Mother's Garden #1 / Encaustic / 16" x 20"

EPILOGUE

. . . Healing, love, and joy

As I mentioned in the introduction, I wrote this book for the fun of sharing many of my artistic efforts. But also, throughout the compilation (because it only seemed natural to do so) I hinted that my art provided me much more than a spate of amusement. For one thing, creativity uplifted me, comforted me, and also seemed to heal my physical ailments. In retrospect, I see that my art has allowed me to relive adventures, recall and be grateful for longtime companionships, and even pay a bit of homage to family and my dear Everett.

All of this leads to my own personal theory: there's a measure of inspiration, hope, comfort, and power whenever anyone applies intentional focus to any sweet and satisfying facet in life. If a person involves a right-brain activity while purposefully concentrating upon those fine things—memories, dear people, splendid vistas, best-loved animals, or sustained friendships—then that determined focus even more assuredly attracts great measures of healing, love, and joy.

I take this as a being fact—a fact I've most happily stumbled upon.

A particularly special piece was the sculpture I made of my dear nephews Jonathan and Andrew, left. I was also pleased with the self-portrait, above, I created in my work with Eric Kaposta—especially the frilly lace neckline that I dreamed up for myself—and very excited to see it fired in Ed Hankey's kiln. However, as is sometimes the case in producing works of clay, it exploded into so many pieces that rebuilding it proved too daunting a task. These are the sorts of things that help us grow and make us stronger. As with so much in life, art is about the journey, not the destination.

ACKNOWLEDGMENTS

—

The person I want to thank most with all my heart is my dear husband, Everett. His love and support made this all possible.

Much gratitude goes out to Tim Connolly at Fenwick Publishing and his design staff for making my book one to cherish forever.

Thanks a million to Sarah Morgans, my editor, who has been one of those angels I have written about in my book. Her years of experience have given me the confidence I needed while writing my book.

During the course of writing my book there have been many dear and precious friends who have been very helpful and supportive throughout the entire process. First, thank you so much to Chris Wyatt for all her assistance and support. I've also been so blessed to have friends who took the time to write their own reflections for my book. Thank you so much Shirley Burns, Julann Campbell, Everett DuBois, Ed Hankey, Heather Hwang, Cookie Joe, Moira McDonough, Helene Reed, Teresa Schultz, Lorie Thompson, Karen Wilson, and Marilyn Woodruff.

This book would never have become a reality if it weren't for the words, "Bernie, you have got to write a book," that echoed in my head from Moira McDonough, Maureen Gilbert, and Debora Simpson. Thank you for your persistence.

My heart is filled with love and gratitude for everyone who has contributed to making my life special.